THE STORY OF THOMAS ALVA
EDISON

Can you imagine having no electric lights or movies or phonographs? That's how it was before one man invented them all.

Thomas Edison left school when he was twelve to sell candy on a railroad train. In between sales he did experiments in the baggage car. Then he learned how to be a telegraph operator and began to invent things. He never stopped. By the end of his amazing career, he had invented the light bulb, motion pictures, the phonograph, had installed New York City's electrical system, and had made improvements in almost every other means of communication in use today. He brought about a revolution in living: people now could work and read after the sun went down, and could hear each other over vast distances.

This is the lively story of the genius who affected the twentieth century more than any other inventor.

THE STORY OF THOMAS ALVA
EDISON

BY MARGARET COUSINS

RANDOM HOUSE ▪ NEW YORK

© Copyright, 1965, by Margaret Cousins
All rights reserved under International and Pan-American Copyright Conventions. Published in the United States by Random House, Inc., New York, and simultaneously in Canada by Random House of Canada Limited, Toronto.

Library of Congress Cataloging in Publication Data:
Cousins, Margaret [Date] The story of Thomas Alva Edison. (Landmark books ; no. 8) Includes index.
SUMMARY: A biography of the great inventor whose creations have contributed to the comfort, convenience, and entertainment of people all over the world.
1. Edison, Thomas A. (Thomas Alva), 1847–1931—Juvenile literature. 2. Inventors—United States—Biography—Juvenile literature. 3. Electric engineers—United States—Biography—Juvenile literature. [1. Edison, Thomas A. (Thomas Alva), 1847–1931. 2. Inventors] I. Title.
[TK140.E3C64 1981] 621.3′092′4 [B] [92] 81–805
ISBN: 0–394–84883–7 (pbk.) AACR2

Illustration credits: Bettmann Archive, 144; Edison National Historic Site, ii, vi, 6, 15, 19, 27, 44, 63, 70, 74, 79, 84, 87, 91, 93, 96, 102, 111, 117, 129, 133, 136, 142, 153, 157, 164, 173; Henry Ford Museum and Greenfield Village, 29, 51; Erik Monberg, drawings on 113 from *The Daily Graphic*, January 3, 1880, and 124–125 from *Harper's Weekly*, June 24, 1882; Elmer Smith, map on 13; Underwood & Underwood, 150, 161, 169.

Manufactured in the United States of America 1 2 3 4 5 6 7 8 9 0

Contents

Thomas A. Edison

"*Everything comes to him who hustles while he waits.*"

—Thomas Alva Edison

1

Youngest Child

Thomas Alva Edison was born in the early morning hours of February 11, 1847, in the bustling little town of Milan, Ohio. His father's neat red-brick house stood on a little rise of ground overlooking the Huron River and the canal that joined the river to Lake Erie. It was drifted deep in snow from a storm which had blown in from the lake. The winter dark was dimly lighted by candles and oil lamps, but the child who was born that day would someday light the lamp that shines around the world.

3

Samuel Edison paced the floor before the closed door of his wife's room. He was a restless man, but he was unusually nervous now. His wife, Nancy, had prayed for this child. The three youngest of their six children had died young in the long, hard winters. Their elder daughter, Marion, was soon to be married. Pitt Edison was going on fifteen. Harriet Ann, better known as Tannie, was thirteen. A baby would make a lot of difference.

Nancy Elliott Edison loved children—all children. She was a sturdy little person, who had been born in Chenango County, New York, but grew up in Canada. Her ancestors were Scottish. Her father was a Baptist minister, who believed that girls should be educated. He sent Nancy to school and she, in turn, taught school before she married Samuel Edison, an innkeeper of Vienna, Ontario. She married at eighteen.

Nancy's life was not easy. Her fiery young husband, who stood six feet one inch without shoes, could outjump, outrun and outfight anybody in his township, and he was always doing just that. He found it hard to settle down to business, so he changed his trade many times. He had a quick temper and a hot head.

He arrived in the United States one jump ahead of the bloodhounds.

Sam Edison, displeased with the politics of the

4

Royal Canadian Government, had joined a rebellion against the government in 1837. The government's victory made Sam Edison a traitor. When the king's soldiers came looking for him, he decided to make a run for the border. He could almost outrun a deer, and he had staying power. He set off at top speed, chased by soldiers, scouts and dogs. He ran for two days without stopping to sleep, skated across the frozen St. Clair River and arrived in Port Huron, Michigan.

When he had caught his breath and looked around, he decided to push on south. A new canal, which made it possible for boats to go from the Huron River into Lake Erie, had just been built at Milan, Ohio. Because Milan was a boom town, Sam Edison decided this would be a good place to sell building materials. He settled in Milan and opened a lumberyard and shingle mill. He built a pretty brick house, with leaded windows, white shutters and a picket fence, and sent for his wife and children.

Sam Edison continued to pace the floor. Finally, the neighbor woman who was caring for his wife opened the door and came out.

"You have a fine boy," she said. "Light hair and blue eyes—the image of his mother!"

"I'm glad he looks like her," Sam Edison said. "If he grows up to act like her, that will be even better!"

The house where Thomas Alva Edison was born

The neighbor smiled. Nancy Edison was known for her sweet nature and gentleness. "I don't know about that," she said, "but I think he's an unusual child. He has a really big head."

When Sam Edison first saw his seventh and last child, the baby's head looked so large that Sam was afraid something was wrong with him.

"Do you think he'll grow to it?" he asked.

"He's perfect!" Nancy said. She adored the boy

from the moment she first saw him, and became his lifelong champion.

They named him Thomas Alva Edison—Thomas for a great-uncle and Alva in honor of Sam's friend Captain Alva Bradley, who operated a fleet of cargo boats on the Great Lakes. The boy was usually called Alva when he was young, and his mother always called him Al.

Little Al started out immediately to prove that he was unusual. To begin with, he almost never cried. He gurgled and laughed all the time. He seemed to see the funny side of everything and seemed to try to make other people laugh too. "Even as a baby, Al cracked jokes," one of his friends said of him years later.

He was very single-minded as a baby. He would fix his attention on some object and then appear to try to figure out how to get hold of it. He would screw up his forehead, as if he were thinking, frown, purse his lips and try to do whatever he had planned. As soon as he learned to walk, he displayed a mind of his own and would walk off by himself after what he wanted.

Alva grew into a handsome boy. His head remained big but well shaped. He had a broad, high, smooth forehead and his light blue eyes looked out from under straight eyebrows. He had a beautiful mouth and a nice nose. But his heavy light hair was a problem. It wouldn't curl. It wouldn't part. It wouldn't lie flat. It stuck up in cowlicks. Nancy Edison, much against her will, was forced to keep it cropped short. At the age of three Alva was already running his fingers through his hair when he was thinking.

If curiosity killed the cat, it is a wonder that Thomas Alva Edison stayed alive. From earliest memory, his curiosity about everything was intense. He seemed to want to learn to talk just so he could ask questions. The minute he learned he began to ask them, and he asked them the rest of his life. Some of his questions were puzzling. Some were deep and hard to answer. And some of them were just silly. But he never stopped asking them. He wore his family out, with the exception of his mother, who always kept her patience.

"Why does the wind blow?" he asked his father.

"I don't know, Al," Sam Edison said.

"Why don't you know?" Alva inquired.

Alva was interested in everything. He seemed to feel that all nature was full of secrets, and it was up to him to find out about them. He was out in the barnyard helping his mother to gather eggs one day when they came on a goose, sitting on her nest.

"Why isn't the goose eating with the rest of the chickens?" Al wanted to know.

"She is sitting on her eggs," his mother said.

"Why?" asked Al.

8

"To keep them warm," his mother said.

"Why does she want to keep them warm?"

"So they'll hatch."

"What's 'hatch'?"

"Geese hatch when the babies peck the shell with their beaks and come out."

"If eggs are kept warm will a goose come out?"

"Well, if it's the right time, and they're goose eggs."

"Oh."

That afternoon Al gave his parents no trouble. He disappeared and they couldn't find him. At sundown his father went looking for him. Sam found Al in a neighbor's barn, squatting on a nest filled with eggs he had gathered. He was discouraged that the goslings hadn't decided to come out!

Al's brother and sisters were so much older that he usually played alone or stayed with his mother. Although he slept in a room without windows under the eaves with Pitt and Tannie, they were too grown-up to spend much time with him. He tried to do everything that Pitt did. When Pitt drew pictures, Al drew pictures. When Pitt read a book, Al tried to read too.

Most of the time he played out in the yard under the kitchen windows, where his mother could keep an eye on him. The minute her eye wandered, so did he. He sprinted for the bank of the canal, running along the tow path behind the

9

six-horse teams that were pulling the boats through the locks to the lake, or picking his way along the docks among the ropes and anchors of the shipyards that lined the canal.

The canal banks made a wonderful place for a boy to play. There were grist mills and grain elevators and tanneries for cattle hides and blacksmith shops. Here the horses stood to be shod. The sparks flew up from the anvil. The clang of hammers rang out as the blacksmith in his leather apron, grimy with soot, shaped the red-hot metal.

It was almost impossible for Al, with his curiosity, not to get in trouble. Once he fell into a pile of wheat chaff in a grain elevator. He almost suffocated before somebody grabbed him by the heels and rescued him. Another time, he fell into the canal and had to be fished out, dripping wet and frightened.

He often visited the flour mill of Sam Winchester, a Yankee inventor, who was experimenting with building a hydrogen balloon. This was no place for a child to play, and he was often warned by his father to stay away. Through Winchester's balloon Al became interested in flight. He mixed a chemical mess which, if swallowed, he was convinced, would make anybody lighter than air. He tried to persuade his father's hired hand, Michael Oates, to take a dose and fly. Michael refused, but Al nagged him so that he finally gave in. He became so ill that a doctor had to be called. Al seemed to think it was Michael's fault, not his, that he didn't fly.

For all these misdeeds, Al was soundly spanked. His father felt that only a good thrashing would cure such a talent for mischief. His mother believed that if you spared the rod you spoiled the child. Al was never spoiled. He took his lickings as a matter of course, and they never stopped his curiosity.

When he was six years old, Al got his worst whipping. He had been playing in his father's barn and he decided to start a small fire. "I just wanted to see what it would do," he said. It is hardly necessary to describe what it did. The flames spread rapidly in all directions. Al managed to get out alive, but the barn burned to the ground and the whole town was in danger of going up in smoke if the wind changed. The offense was too terrible and too dangerous to be ignored. Al confessed to the crime of arson. But you cannot put a six-year-old boy in jail.

Samuel Edison announced that he would whip his son, Alva, in the public square to teach him a lesson. He invited the townspeople to come and watch. Children were whipped regularly in those days, both at home and in school, but it was unheard of to make a public display. However, the townspeople came and brought their children, to teach *them* a lesson. Sam Edison flogged his young son before their eyes. Alva did not harbor anger against his father. After that, he never seemed much impressed by pain—his own or other people's.

About the same time Al was involved in another tragedy. He had gone to a creek to swim with a boy his own age. While they were playing in the water, the other boy disappeared down the creek. Alva waited for him to come back. But when it began to get late and the boy did not come, Al went on home. He never thought to mention his friend. In the middle of the night he was awakened and asked about the boy.

"I waited and waited," Al said. "He didn't come."

The boy had drowned. Al did not understand that he should have mentioned his friend's disappearance, but his father began to think of him as a problem child. Samuel was afraid his son had no feelings.

When Al was seven years old, his father's business in Milan began to decline. As the railroads pushed north, shipping on the canal grew less and less. A depression settled on the whole town. Samuel Edison decided to move. He remembered the pretty little town of Port Huron, in Michigan, where he had entered the United States.

Port Huron stood at the entrance of Lake

Huron from the St. Clair River. Sam Edison rented a house on the northern edge of the town at Fort Gratiot, an old French trading post. It was a big, strong house with columned porches, in a grove of pines on ten acres of ground. It had views of the lake and the river. The rooms of the house were large and there were four big fireplaces. There were an apple orchard and a garden, barns and other buildings.

The Edisons, packing up their household goods, took a train and then a carriage to Detroit. Next they boarded a paddle boat, which took them up the St. Clair River to their new home.

Before Al had time to get acquainted with Port Huron, he came down with scarlet fever. He was very ill and did not recover rapidly. It is quite possible that this illness affected his ears. His mother did not send him to school that year. He went on playing by himself and staying with his mother, who loved to have him near.

About this time, Samuel Edison hit upon the idea of building a wooden observation tower, a hundred feet high, on his hill overlooking the surrounding scenery. He was in the lumber and feed business in Port Huron and thought the tower would be a good advertisement. For twenty-five cents, visitors could climb the tower and look at the view through a telescope on the top platform. Al was gatekeeper and collected the quarters. When the railroad came to Port Huron,

Edison at about eight years old, with his sister Tannie

excursionists often visited the tower, which was called Edison's Tower of Babel. But the tower sometimes swayed in the wind and frightened nervous people on the stairs. And gradually the novelty wore off. Al and his mother often climbed the tower together and sat there looking at the lake and river and talking as if they were the same age.

Because of moving and getting settled and his scarlet fever, Al didn't start to school until he was eight years old. He went to a country school, with all the classes in one room, taught by a minister and his wife, the Reverend and Mrs. G. B. Engle. Most of the teaching was done by giving the pupils things to memorize—the alphabet, the multiplication tables, dates in history. Al liked to ask why and receive answers rather than just memorizing what was in front of him. He wanted the arithmetic explained to him. He did not get along well in the school and was always at the foot of his class.

After about three months in the school, one day he heard Mr. Engle say: "That Edison boy is addled. He can't learn."

Al was a quiet, good-natured boy, but the unfairness of this made his blood boil. He grabbed his hat and coat and ran home.

"I will never go back to that school," he announced.

When his mother finally persuaded him to tell

her what had happened, she was even angrier than he was. The next morning she put on her bonnet and paid a call on the Reverend Mr. Engle.

"I understand you think my son is backward," Nancy Edison said.

"He doesn't pay attention to his lessons," the teacher said.

"I have taught school myself," Al's mother told Engle, "and I believe I am in position to say that he is brighter than most boys his age." Nancy Edison went on to imply that there must be something wrong with the Engles' teaching methods.

Engle then suggested that mother love might blind her to the facts.

Nancy Edison drew herself up. "I will teach Al myself," she said. "He won't be coming here anymore!"

Al went to school only three months of his life. After that time, his mother took charge of his education. He studied every day on a regular schedule not only in the winter but also in the summer, when the other boys were skylarking on vacation. He did not mind, because his mother gave him not only learning but the love of learning. She believed that it was more important to reason than to memorize.

Nancy Edison's method was to read aloud to Al the best books she could find—the plays of

Shakespeare, the novels of Dickens and many important works of history. At the age of eight, Al became interested in reading good books, and by the time he was nine he could read advanced books very rapidly. He had to learn to do everything himself. Unfortunately, he never learned accurate spelling and punctuation, which require a certain amount of memorizing. He learned to add and subtract, and to multiply and divide, but he never seemed to get very interested in arithmetic. He looked at numbers another way.

"I'm a bushel of wheat," he said to his mother one day.

"What makes you say that?" she asked.

"I weigh eighty pounds," he said.

When Al was nine years old he read a science textbook containing some experiments that could be performed at home. This opened a whole new world to him. He tried out all the suggestions in the book. His mother bought him the *Dictionary of Science.* After that, all his allowance went to buy chemicals at the drugstore. He collected old wire and scrap metal to use in his experiments. His room was a mess, since the chemicals sometimes exploded or acid ran out of bottles and ate up the carpet.

Nancy Edison finally did lose patience and told Al that he had to move all those dreadful bottles and smelly jars—two hundred in all—out of the

Samuel and Nancy Edison

bedroom. Alva found a corner in the cellar where he set up his first laboratory. He was ten years old. After he got his laboratory ready, his mother could hardly persuade him to come upstairs to meals. He always locked the door of the cellar when he left.

Sometimes Al's father would bribe him to read a book that wasn't about chemistry. Al would read anything to get another penny to buy more chemicals at the drugstore. Anyway, he liked to read. He had already read, before he was ten years old, Hume's *History of England*, Gibbon's *Decline and Fall of the Roman Empire* and Sears'

19

History of the World. Then he read *The Age of Reason* by Thomas Paine.

When Thomas Alva Edison was young, people were as much interested in electricity as we are now in outer space. The existence of electricity had been known for many centuries. The ancient Greeks knew that if you rubbed a piece of amber, it assumed a new property—the ability to attract particles of other substances. In 1600 A.D. a scientist named William Gilbert studied this phenomenon, which was called electricity, from the Greek word for amber. In the next 250 years, many scientists studied electricity and added to the knowledge about it. Benjamin Franklin proved that lightning is an electrical discharge. In the thirty years before Edison's birth, Georg Simon Ohm in Germany and Michael Faraday in England made important contributions to the science of electricity.

Al Edison, who had an inquiring mind, became interested in electricity through the telegraph, which was an exciting new discovery when he was a boy. The electric telegraph was invented by Samuel F. B. Morse, an artist who lived in New York. Morse started work on his telegraph idea in 1832, applied for a patent in 1837 and received it in 1840. In 1844, three years before Edison was born, Congress gave money to Morse to lay a telegraph wire between Washington and Baltimore.

The Morse telegraph sent messages over a wire by alternately making and breaking an electric circuit. When the sending operator pressed a key, a switch closed the circuit for a moment. Electric current then flowed to a sounder at the receiving end. The sounder used an electromagnet to attract an iron bar. The electromagnet was an iron rod wrapped with many turns of wire connected to a battery. When the current flowed for a moment through the coiled wire, it magnetized the rod, and the sounder's iron bar was pulled down against the magnet, making a loud click.

Morse invented a code with short and long signals—dots and dashes—for letters, numbers and punctuation marks. The sender tapped out words and sentences in Morse code. The receiving operator at the other end took down the code signals and translated them into words.

The railroads seized on this invention and began to make use of it at once. Communication between stations was very important to them. It increased the efficiency of their rolling stock (locomotives and train cars), reduced accidents, and enabled railroads to improve their schedules. They began to lay wires along their rights-of-way. Stations installed telegraph keys, and station agents learned the Morse code.

Communication beyond the range of the human voice had been going on since prehistoric times. Some African tribes used drumbeats. The American Indians used signal fires. But when Al was a boy, people had just begun to be able to send messages great distances—by use of an electric circuit in a wire. No wonder he was excited and wanted to understand how these great new developments were possible.

By the time Al was eleven years old, the telegraph was operating between New York and Boston and even as far west as Chicago. The newspapers were full of stories of the telegraph pioneers who were stringing wires across the wild continent. It was Edison's ambition to be a telegrapher.

At the age of eleven he had his first homemade telegraph set, which he built from a description in a science book. He strung picture wire between two houses, through the woods and through a tunnel under the street. The electro-magnets were wound with wire, and the key was a piece of brass.

In an effort to generate electric current, Edison got two cats, attached a wire to their legs, and applied friction to their backs by rubbing them. The experiment was a great failure. The cats refused to cooperate and took to spitting and clawing before they ran off. The telegraph line had to be temporarily abandoned.

The failure of this experiment did not discourage Al; it redoubled his determination to build a successful Morse sending-and-receiving telegraph set. But he needed money. Samuel Edison's business had not been good and the family had no money for anything but necessities. Al sat down to figure out how to get some cash. He decided to go into the truck-farming business. He and Michael Oates, the hired hand, laid out a large garden on one of Samuel Edison's acres. They planted onions, cabbages, peas, beans, lettuce and corn, which they hoed and weeded in the hot sun. Then they rented a horse and wagon and sold the vegetables from door to door in Port Huron. They earned several hundred dollars that way, but they turned over most of the money to Al's mother.

Hoeing corn seemed to Al to be a waste of time. He heard there was an opening on the new railroad from Detroit to Port Huron for a boy to sell sandwiches and fruit and candy to the passengers. Al decided to apply for the job. There was no salary paid, but the "candy butcher" could buy his goods, peddle them for a profit and keep the profit.

Al was only twelve years old and young for the job. His mother was against the whole idea. She imagined train wrecks in which Al would be pinned beneath the twisted cars. She worried about his getting into bad company during the long wait between trains in Detroit. But Al's father, who saw no hope of sending his son to school, said that Al could improve his mind while he was waiting for the return train in Detroit. Al thought only of making money to buy things for his scientific experiments.

The Edison family probably needed the few dollars he would be able to turn over to them. Al finally talked his mother into letting him try to be a candy butcher, and the Grand Trunk Railway gave him the job.

At the age of twelve his childhood was over.

2

Enterprising Newsboy

When he started his business career, Al Edison
was a middle-sized boy, strong and well built,
with light blue eyes and a thick head of brown
hair, which he hardly ever combed. He always
had trouble keeping his hair in order, and soon
gave up. He had a large, open face, a square jaw
and a wide, well-shaped mouth. He dressed in
shabby clothes and seemed to take no interest in
his looks. He had one cheap suit which he wore
until it was threadbare, and then he bought
another one. His mother forced him to wash his

hands and face and wear clean shirts, but nobody seemed able to persuade him to shine his shoes. He wore a round, short-peaked cap and usually had a big scarf wound around his neck to keep him warm.

In spite of not caring how he looked, Al was very good-looking. His eyes were bright and full of fun. He wanted to be doing something all the time and he never got tired. He could sleep anywhere. A few minutes of sleep seemed to do as much for him as hours did for other people. He was already absent-minded, for even when he was with other people he was usually thinking of some scheme and how to make it work. He would take part in a conversation or play a game of checkers, but his mind was often somewhere else.

Al soon figured out that, if he had a helper on his train run, he could share profits with his employee and still come out ahead. He hired a boy named Barney Maisonville to work for him on Saturdays when there was no school. Even at the age of twelve, Al Edison delegated details to others.

The baggage car of the train had a compartment for mail and a compartment for baggage. On such a short run as between Port Huron and

Edison at fourteen

Detroit, there was never much baggage. So Al took over the empty space in the baggage compartment for his office.

The first Saturday he showed Barney how to peddle the fruit and candy. After that he expected Barney to carry out his instructions without being reminded. Barney rarely saw Al on the train, as Al had turned his office into a laboratory and was usually working on an experiment.

Al left Port Huron at 7:00 in the morning, arriving in Detroit at 10:30 a.m. The return train left Detroit at 4:30 in the afternoon and arrived in Port Huron at 7:30 in the evening. During the six hours in Detroit, Al bought his goods to sell on the train—bananas, oranges, candy, peanuts, newspapers and magazines—and carried them to the baggage car. If there was any time left over, in Detroit, he went to the Free Library or read a book—he always carried one in his pocket.

Al made a favorable impression on the men who supplied him with goods. They all thought him young to be such a good merchant. It was from one of these men that he bought his first printing press—a small hand press with a supply of type that the man had used to print menus for hotels and restaurants. It was such a bargain Al couldn't resist it. He installed the press in his baggage-car office, along with his laboratory.

On Saturdays, he and Barney did the chores together. Al paid for their dinner at the Cass

House, Detroit's good hotel. When Barney turned over his receipts at the end of the day, Al never bothered to count the money. He simply put it in his pocket.

"Why don't you count it?" Barney asked.

"I'm sure it's all right," Al said.

He was never able to get very much interested

Replica of the railway baggage car that served as young Edison's office and laboratory

in money—only in what it would buy. He trusted people until they proved they could not be trusted. During this time he was also operating a vegetable market and a newspaper stand in Port Huron. He closed the newspaper stand when the boy he had hired cheated him. He kept the vegetable market going until his newspaper business on the train picked up.

The Civil War brought Al his first wealth as a newsboy. One day in April 1862, he saw a crowd of people gathered around a bulletin board in Detroit, where news about the Battle of Shiloh was posted. This gave Al an idea. He hurried to the railroad station and persuaded the telegrapher there to flash the rumor about the terrible casualties of the battle to the stations along the route to Port Huron, asking that the news be posted on station bulletin boards.

Al then raced to the *Detroit Free Press* office, determined to buy a thousand papers. He usually bought a hundred. And he had money enough to pay for only three hundred. But he decided to buy them on credit. He asked for the editor-in-chief. When he was shown into the editor's office, there were two men there.

"I believe I can sell a thousand papers with news of the Battle of Shiloh," Edison said. "But I will have to buy seven hundred of them on credit."

The editor said it would be ridiculous to extend

that much credit to a fifteen-year-old boy. But the other man, Wilbur F. Storey, managing editor of the paper, persuaded the editor to let Al have the papers. They told him he would have to get them to the train himself.

Al hired a boy off the street and carried the papers to the Grand Trunk baggage car, where he started folding them. It wasn't Saturday, so Barney wasn't with him.

At Utica, Michigan, a tiny town that was the first stop out of Detroit, he saw the platform was crowded with people. He paid no attention, thinking maybe it was an excursion crowd. But when the train stopped and Al jumped down, the crowd swarmed toward him. They had read the telegraphed notice and were fighting for the newspapers. He sold thirty-five papers before the train started, at the regular price of five cents each. Usually he sold two papers in Utica. The same stampede took place at Mount Clemens and at every stop on the line. Al decided to raise the price of the papers. By the time he got to Port Huron, he had only a few left.

Al usually left the train before it got to the Port Huron station. While the train was still moving, he jumped off into a pile of sand he had hauled to the spot to land in. His friend Michael Oates met him there with a horse and wagon and he got home more quickly. On this day, he bundled up his remaining papers and jumped. When the wagon got to the outskirts of Port Huron, a great crowd met them, clamoring for papers.

"They're twenty-five cents apiece, gentlemen," Al yelled. "I haven't got enough to go around."

As he passed a church where a prayer meeting was going on, the entire congregation came out of the church and began to bid against each other for the papers. Some people paid a dollar for one paper. The reports of casualties at Shiloh were so great that nothing seemed more important than reading the casualty lists.

Al sold all his papers. When he got home, his pockets were bulging with money.

Al always gave his mother one dollar out of each day's receipts, but that day he gave her nearly a hundred dollars. He spent the rest of the money for chemicals to stock his baggage-car laboratory.

The success of this venture gave Al another idea. He made friends with one of the men who set type at the *Detroit Free Press*. Every day he went to see this man, who showed him the first proof of the most important news story of the day. Al would then ask his telegrapher friend in Detroit to flash the news ahead to the railroad stations on his route. He soon learned to gauge the number of papers he could sell by the importance of the news.

Al's success as a seller of newspapers encour-

aged him to start a paper of his own, using the
hand press he had bought. In his baggage-car
office, he wrote the news, set the type and
printed the *Weekly Herald,* which was much
smaller in size than a regular newspaper. The
paper contained local news and gossip. Al sold it
for eight cents a month and it had a circulation of
about four hundred—mostly the men who
worked on and around the railroad. The paper
told about engines that were being repaired,
porters who had done good jobs, accidents to
men on the line, marriages and babies, notices of
lost luggage and schedules of the stage coaches
that met the trains. It also contained jokes and
editorials. The paper had a good many misspelled
words, grammatical errors and unusual punctuation, but nobody seemed to mind. It was the first
newspaper ever published on a train.

The success of the *Weekly Herald* persuaded Al
and a friend of his to start a real gossip sheet
called *Paul Pry.* This paper was more amusing to
the people whose names did not appear in it than
to those who were written up. Al and his victims
knew nothing about libel, but one of the promi-
nent citizens of Port Huron took offense at an
item about him in *Paul Pry.* He met the young
editor on the Port Huron docks one evening,
grabbed him by the scruff of the neck and threw
him into the St. Clair River. Fortunately, Al was a
strong swimmer. Immediately afterward and

probably at the command of his father, *Paul Pry* suspended publication.

About the same time the baggage-car laboratory came to an end. One day while Al was experimenting in the laboratory, the jolting of the old baggage car upset a bottle of phosphorus which fell on the floor and set the car afire. While Al was trying to beat out the flames, Alexander Stevenson, the conductor, arrived. Stevenson, who had always been friendly to Al, had good reason to be upset. The floor of his baggage car was in flames. The minute he got the fire put out, he boxed Al's ears.

Al kept his job as candy butcher on the Grand Trunk. He continued to publish the *Herald* for a while in a workshop his father gave him. Alexander Stevenson resigned shortly after the incident.

In many books about Edison, Stevenson's blows have been reported as responsible for the inventor's near deafness. In actual fact, Al had been hard of hearing for about two years when this happened. He was thirteen when he first noticed that he could not hear well. One morning he was late to the train, and as he was running along trying to board the moving railroad car, a trainman grabbed him by his ears and lifted him aboard.

"I felt something snap inside my head," Edison said, "and the deafness started from that time."

Doctors think that his hearing had probably

been affected by his severe attack of scarlet fever, and that any blow on the head may have added to the problem. His deafness has been diagnosed as arthritis of the small bones of the ear. Edison wrote many years later: "I haven't heard a bird sing since I was twelve years old."

His deafness may be one reason why he never went back to school. From the age of twelve he could not hear the teachers. He could hear the grinding noises of the locomotive and the train cars and the voices of people shouting at each other above the racket. But he could not hear ordinary conversation. His hearing grew worse the longer he lived. But he never complained.

The fact that he was hard of hearing drove him to even more reading and study. Every day while he waited for the afternoon train, he went to the Detroit Free Library and read the next book on the shelf. He started with books whose titles began with A and read through Z—fifteen feet of books. One of his favorite writers was Victor Hugo, and he read every one of Hugo's novels. He talked about this writer so often that his friends nicknamed him Victor Hugo Edison.

Another favorite place of Al's during the daily layover in Detroit was the machine shop of the Grand Trunk Railway. He loved to walk around the yards and talk to the mechanics and engineers and hitch rides in the cab of a switch engine (that moved cars from one track to another). He loved the big locomotives with their bright brass bands, their painted woodwork and all their polished parts. It was his ambition to run an engine.

Once when Al was riding a slow freight train, the engineer and the fireman, who had been to a dance the night before, became so sleepy they couldn't keep their eyes open. They decided to let Al run the engine and retired to the caboose to nap.

"I was worried about the water," Al said later. "I knew if it got low the boiler might explode. I hadn't gone twenty miles when a pile of black, damp mud blew out of the smokestack and covered every part of the engine, including me. When we got to the next station, I did what the fireman always did. I went to the cow-catcher to open the oil cup on the steam chest and pour oil in. When I opened the oil cup, the steam rushed out with a big noise, nearly knocking me off the engine. I succeeded in closing the oil cup and got back in the cab and made up my mind she would pull through without oil. I learned afterward that the engineer always shut off the steam when the fireman went to oil!"

Before he got where he was going, a second shower of mud covered him. He found then that he was carrying too much water. The dampness had gotten into the smokestack and loosened a whole mass of soot, which covered him and the engine with a fine, greasy black powder. This ended Al's active career as an engineer. But, years later, as we shall see, he was a pioneer in developing the electric locomotive.

Al and his friend Michael continued to get into scrapes. During the Civil War, troops were stationed at Fort Gratiot, near Edison's home. Although he was hard of hearing, Al could hear the line of sentries bellowing out the calls that summoned the corporal of the guard in case something was wrong. It occurred to Al and Michael that they could have some fun. One dark night, they bellowed an imitation of the first sentry, and the second sentry took it up. The call went all the way down the line. Out trotted the corporal to run a half-mile along the line of sentries—to find nothing.

The boys were so delighted with watching the frustration of the guard that they repeated the hoax the next night. Once more it worked. But by the third night, the corporal and the sentries had figured out the joke. They were ready for their tormentors. They grabbed Michael and put him in the Fort Gratiot guardhouse. Al, who was more nimble, got away.

"They chased me clear home," he later said. "I rushed for the cellar. In one small compartment there were two barrels of potatoes and another barrel nearly empty. I poured the remnants of one into the other barrels. Then I sat down

37

and pulled the empty barrel over my head, bottom up.

"The soldiers awakened my father, and they were searching for me with candles and lanterns. The corporal was absolutely certain I came into the cellar, and couldn't see how I could have got out, and wanted to know from my father if there was no secret hiding place. On assurance of my father, who said there was not, he said it was most extraordinary. I was glad when they left, as I was cramped, and the potatoes in the barrel were rotten and extremely offensive."

The next morning Michael Oates got out of jail and Al got the usual punishment—a good whipping. This ended their career of teasing the army.

One of their scrapes was international. When the Prince of Wales, who later became King Edward VII, visited Canada and the United States, there was a great public welcome for the prince at Sarnia, Ontario, just across the St. Clair River from Port Huron. Everybody in Port Huron went, including Al and his friends.

They were quite disappointed when they saw the prince, who turned out to be just a young man. The Yankee boys announced to the Canadian boys that their prince wasn't much. A quarrel began immediately, and the boys from each side of the border tangled in a fist fight.

"We were badly licked," Edison remembered later. "I got a black eye!"

Al used some of his earnings as a newsboy to improve his homemade telegraph equipment. But he didn't have much time to study this new science, because he worked from 7:00 in the morning until 7:30 at night, and his father made him go to bed at 9:30. Al always brought his father the papers he hadn't sold, and his father would sit up reading until midnight. Edison tried to point out long, interesting news stories and articles to take his father's mind off the 9:30 curfew, but Samuel Edison always heard the clock strike and sent his son off to bed.

"As the half hour approached, his eye would wander toward the clock, and at the tick, I would hear his voice yelling at me to go to bed, and off I went," Al recalled later.

"My friend, Dick, who was also interested in telegraphy, and I had a homemade line strung between our two houses. We had learned how to send and take messages in Morse code. But we didn't have time to practice, because I had to go to bed. One day on the train Dick and I figured out how to get around this rule of my father's. I didn't take any newspapers home with me. That night, when my father asked me for one, I said: 'Dick's got them all. He took them to his house. His folks wanted them.' That took him back a bit but I didn't say any more until I was going to bed. Then I made a suggestion: 'Dick and I have a telegraph line working between our rooms,' I said. 'Maybe I could call him and get the news by wire.' "

Sam Edison was doubtful, but he wanted to know the news of the day. So Al called Dick, who sat in front of his instrument with the paper before him and tapped out the news in Morse code. Al took it down on slips of paper and passed it over to his father to read as fast as each news item was finished. That night Al got to stay up until eleven o'clock, feeding his father the events of the day in small doses. This went on for several days until Sam Edison was convinced it did Al no harm to stay up until eleven o'clock. After that Al brought his father the papers again and used his extra time to experiment with the telegraph.

Al and his friends finally had a network of telegraph lines strung among a dozen houses. They sent and received messages at all times of the day and night. Al did most of the work of building the lines. He began by stringing the wires from tree to tree and insulating them with the necks of broken bottles. Later he put up small poles which made the sending and receiving clearer. This system worked until a stray cow got loose in the Edison orchard, knocked down a half-dozen poles, got tangled up in the wires and began to bellow in terror. Finally some of the family went out to set her free. Al never repaired those lines.

True to his mother's worries, he was finally in a

train wreck. About a week before Christmas, when he had laid in extra stocks of Christmas candles, dates, raisins, apples and oranges, the Grand Trunk jumped the track. Four old cars were smashed, and Al's figs, dates and candy were strewn all over the railroad right of way.

Al wasn't hurt, but he could not bear to see his candy and fruit go to waste. He couldn't sell wrecked Christmas stock, so he tried eating what he could pick up along the track.

"That night our family doctor had the time of his life with me!" Edison later said. He had such a stomach ache that the physician had to be summoned. Nobody could understand what he had eaten to make him so sick. They blamed his illness on the train wreck.

3

Tramp Telegrapher

When Thomas Edison was fifteen years old, something happened that had a lasting effect on his life. One hot August morning in 1862, he was standing on the platform in Mount Clemens while the mixed train of passenger coaches and boxcars took on water and engaged in a half-hour of switching boxcars in the railroad yards. As Al watched the big cars being shunted around, he saw a loaded boxcar without a brakeman leave a siding and come onto the main track, gathering speed. Suddenly Al noticed a small child playing

42

in the gravel at the side of the track. He recognized the little boy as the son of J. U. Mackenzie, the Mount Clemens station agent. Throwing down his papers, Al tore across the track, grabbed the child and swung him out of the way, just as the heavy boxcar rushed past them.

Al carried the frightened child to his father. Mackenzie was so upset he could scarcely speak and mumbled his thanks while trying to quiet his son. Al thought nothing more about the matter. He had done, he thought, what anybody would do. But Mackenzie never forgot it.

Mackenzie thought for several days about what he could do to reward the boy. One morning as Al was going through Mount Clemens, Mackenzie spoke to him about it.

"How would you like to learn telegraphy?" he asked.

"Would I!" Al said.

"I have been wanting to do something for the young man who saved my son's life," Mackenzie said. "I will give you lessons myself."

Al was terribly excited about this plan. They arranged that he would drop off the train at Mount Clemens four evenings a week to study.

When Al arrived for his first lesson, Mackenzie was surprised and pleased to find that the boy was carrying a set of telegraph instruments that he had had made by a Detroit gunsmith.

For five months Al was an apprentice to

The railroad station where young Edison saved a child's life

Mackenzie. He learned all the abbreviated signals used by railroad operators. Telegraphy was a
new trade and there were not many people who
could send and receive messages. The expert's
speed of taking messages was forty-five words a
minute. This took practice but, once mastered, it
meant a job almost anywhere.

At the end of five months Mackenzie said: "You
know as much about telegraphy as I do now, Al. I
can't teach you any more."

Al went back to Port Huron, looking for a job.

The first thing he did was to rent a little office space in the drugstore and string a wire from the Port Huron railroad station to the main street of the town. He planned to send telegrams for people and take the profit. But since telegrams were not in wide general use, this business did not pay for itself. There was already another telegraph office in Port Huron, in the store of Thomas Walker, a jeweler and watchmaker who also sold books and magazines. Walker planned to enlist in the army, so Al was given the job of running the store and the telegraph office.

Al enjoyed himself there because he could read Walker's books and amuse himself with Walker's watchmaking equipment. He moved a cot into the back of the store. He knew everything that happened before anyone else, because he could cut in on the wire to take down dispatches going to the local newspapers. But Walker could afford to pay him only twenty dollars a month. Samuel Edison wouldn't let his son sign apprentice papers for such a small amount. Al had made more money as a candy butcher and newsboy than he first earned as a telegraph operator.

Al applied for a job as telegrapher on the Grand Trunk Railway and became a full-fledged night operator at the age of seventeen. There is a story about how he got this job. During a hard freeze in the winter of 1864, an ice jam broke the telegraph cable under the St. Clair River, between Port Huron and Sarnia. The ferries could not cross through the ice, so all communication was cut off. Al Edison suggested to the railroad men that they run a locomotive down to the Port Huron docks and have the engineer blow the whistle in the Morse code under his direction. They decided to try it, and the long and short blasts of the whistle soon attracted a crowd on the Canadian side. The railroad telegrapher in Sarnia got the idea. A locomotive was brought down to the Sarnia docks and the two towns were back in communication. This feat attracted the attention of the Grand Trunk officials.

Al was assigned to the station at Stratford Junction, Ontario—about a hundred miles from his home town. He would make twenty-five dollars a month and would work from 7 p.m. to 7 a.m. He moved to Stratford Junction and began his career as a telegraph operator.

And he began to be known as Tom. He was no longer little Al.

Tom was not a great success at his first real job in telegraphy. Though he was used to staying up late at night, he couldn't get into the habit of sleeping in the daytime. His work required him to be on the job all night, but there wasn't much to do except to wait for messages that didn't come very often and to signal trains or stations on a regular schedule. Edison took clocks apart to see what made them tick, read books and rigged up little experiments during the night. He also took a few catnaps.

The Grand Trunk Railway required operators to send in the signal for "6" every hour after 9 p.m., to be sure they stayed on duty. Telegraphers in that time were a wild lot—a roving, restless group of tramps, who traveled around the country enjoying themselves with drinking and gambling. They could not always be depended on.

In order not to have to interrupt his research or his naps, Tom rigged up a clock with a notched wheel on the telegraph key, which automatically sent out his signal "6" at the proper time. One night after the "6" signal came through from Stratford Junction, sharp and clear, a train man tried to send a message *to* Stratford Junction. He tried for a long time but nothing happened. Edison did not wake up. An hour later the "6" signal went through again, and the train man decided to investigate. He found the young operator sound asleep.

Edison received a warning.

Shortly after that, he received a message to hold a freight train at Stratford Junction. Before he could get the signal set to stop the train, it roared through the station. Tom ran into the office and reported what had happened. But a dispatcher had already sent another train from the next station in the other direction.

Edison was terrified. He had visions of the two trains meeting in a head-on collision. There was a lower station near the junction where the day operator slept. Tom dashed out of the station and started for it on foot. In the darkness, he stumbled and fell into a ditch, knocking himself unconscious.

Tragedy was averted because the engineers of both trains pulled their locomotives to a stop before they collided, but the railroad investigated. Tom was called to Toronto to explain his actions to W. J. Spicer, the general manager of the Grand Trunk Railroad. While Mr. Spicer was questioning him, he had to stop and greet some visitors. Tom decided to leave the room to get some air. He never went back. He hurried to the railroad yards and hopped a freight to Sarnia. He then hustled onto the ferry and made his way to Port Huron. Tom, like his father before him, left Canada in a hurry.

Tom got his next job with the Lake Shore and Michigan Southern Railway, as night operator at Adrian, Michigan. This job paid seventy-five dollars a month. He was fired for insubordination. He then moved on to Fort Wayne, where he was fired for lack of discipline. Tom could not fit himself into the routines of an office and he was stubborn. If he thought the message he was receiving or sending was more important than the manager's, he would cut into the manager's wire. If he got interested in a book or some gadget he was working on, he would let messages pile up for hours. He was still fond of practical jokes and he did not have much sense about choosing the victims of these jokes. None of these traits made him popular with his bosses.

But the Civil War had drained many of the best telegraphers from the telegraph offices, and jobs were easy to get. From Fort Wayne, Tom wandered to Indianapolis. There he got a job one cold day in November by stopping the Western Union superintendent, John F. Wallick, on the street and asking for work. He was assigned to Union Station.

The Western Union Telegraph Company was a growing commercial organization, backed by important financial interests. It sold its services to the railroads and the newspapers. It owned by this time 25,000 miles of telegraph wire and was reputed to have control of the newspaper wires through its affiliation with Associated Press. Western Union was also involved through its financiers with the railroads. Although there were other telegraph companies in operation, Western Union was striving toward monopoly. A number of congressmen thought it should become government property and be made part of the postal system. This did not happen. But the company did provide a unified telegraph service and encouraged inventors by paying them for their efforts.

During his years as a tramp telegrapher, Tom Edison usually worked for Western Union. His skill and speed at sending and receiving telegrams increased, and he was almost always able to get a job at the Western Union office in any town he decided to move to.

Tom still spent most of his money on electrical equipment, which he carried with him in an old valise. His pockets were always sagging with pliers, coils of wire, metal scraps and splicing materials. As soon as he had rented a cheap hall bedroom in a new town, he would lay out his tools and start a laboratory. On payday he usually spent his entire salary on this sort of equipment and had to borrow money to buy his supper.

Most of Tom's experiments as a wandering telegrapher were concerned with working on a duplex telegraph—a machine which would send two messages in opposite directions at the same time. His habit of making use of the equipment in the telegraph office where he was working to further his experiments was one reason he was fired so often from the job. Managers wanted a telegraph operator, not an experimenter.

Edison at seventeen or eighteen

51

Tom still paid little attention to his clothes. His old suits hung on him, for he had lost weight on boardinghouse food. He wore soiled paper collars and a straw hat even in the winter. His hair still stuck up in cowlicks and he continued to run his hands through it and muss it up. He looked like a country hick. His deafness made him lonesome and shy. The offices where he worked were dreary places in tumble-down buildings, and the rooms he rented were dingy and ugly and often full of bed bugs.

Telegraph equipment at the time was shoddy and so poorly insulated that receiving was far from perfect. Edison often had to make up some of the news he received over the wire. He took every opportunity to increase his speed. He offered to relieve the regular newspaper operator in Indianapolis. He would stay in the office late at night and beg to relieve the night operator. He was soon able to send messages with lightning rapidity and he also became an expert receiver. In Indianapolis he was promoted from the rank of "plug" to first-rate operator. He stayed there until the following February, when he quit his job, packed up his smelly laboratory and went to Cincinnati. He was eighteen years old.

In Cincinnati, Tom met his first good friend among telegraphers, a young man named Milton F. Adams. Adams dressed like a dandy and had a carefree, happy nature and a taste for society.

Cincinnati was the largest city Tom had ever worked in, and here he had his first taste of the theater, museums and great libraries with Milt Adams.

After the Civil War was over, Tom went to Memphis, a city still occupied by the Union Army and in need of telegraphers. The pay was higher. He got $125 a month. But the manager took a dislike to him and said he made trouble in the office. Once again he was fired.

Tom, as usual, had no money and no overcoat. It was the middle of winter. He hitched a ride on a freight train, then walked to Nashville, a distance of 150 miles. There he got a railroad pass to Louisville. He arrived in a snowstorm in his linen duster, a lightweight coat usually worn in summer to protect clothing from dust when driving a horse. He also wore a straw hat.

"I'll never forget the sensation I created, walking through the snowstorm in my airy apparel," he later said.

When he applied for a job in Louisville, the manager asked Edison about his speed. Tom sat down at the key and made it hum, so he got the job. He stayed in Louisville for more than a year. He stopped running around with wild telegraphers and made friends with newspapermen with whom he discussed science and philosophy. He invented a special penmanship, a sort of shorthand, which made his reception of messages

53

faster. He tried to teach himself Spanish.

His mind was full of ideas and schemes, and it was in Louisville that Tom Edison first dreamed of becoming an inventor. He worked feverishly at developing a duplex telegraph. But he could not get enough money to carry out his ideas, and he had begun to despise the monotony of his job.

One day at an auction room, Tom bought for two dollars a great stack of bound volumes of the *North American Review*. The bundle was almost too big to carry, but he dragged it over to the telegraph office where he had to stay on duty until three o'clock in the morning. Then he finally started home with his bundle through the dark streets. He could hardly wait to start reading his books.

"Stop!" a voice shouted, but because he was almost deaf Tom did not hear.

When a pistol shot whizzed past his ear, he heard that. As he turned around an angry policeman rushed up. Believing that Tom had stolen the package, he shouted at him to drop it. Tom laid down his bundle and explained what he was carrying.

"Open it up!" the policeman ordered.

Tom did so and the old books fell out.

"Why didn't you stop when I hollered?" the cop asked, disgusted. "If I'd been a better shot, I'd have killed you."

"I didn't hear you," Tom said. "I'm almost deaf."

The policeman apologized. "You'd better stay off the streets at night," he added.

"I'm a night telegraph operator," Tom said with a grin.

"Well," said the policeman. "I've got no more advice!"

With two ex-Confederate telegraph operators he had met in Louisville, Tom decided to go to South America and become a telegraph operator in Brazil. With his friends, he left Louisville for New Orleans, where they were going to take a ship to Brazil. They arrived in New Orleans during mob riots against the carpetbaggers (adventurers who swarmed into the South after the Civil War) and this delayed the vessel's sailing. By the time the ship sailed, fortunately, Edison had changed his mind. His friends went on and they both died on the way of yellow fever.

Late in 1867 Tom returned to his home in Port Huron for a few months. His father had again fallen on hard times. The Edison house had been confiscated by the military and had become part of Fort Gratiot, forcing the family to move to temporary quarters. His mother was ill and some people said she was losing her mind.

Tom was considered the black sheep of the family. He had no job and no money. But he was very unhappy in Port Huron and decided he had to get away again.

His friend from Cincinnati days, Milton Adams, was living in Boston. He wrote Tom to come there and try for a job. There were several firms manufacturing electrical supplies in Boston. Tom made up his mind to go. It was a long way from Michigan to Massachusetts and he didn't feel like walking. He did some repair work for the railroad in Port Huron and got a pass to Boston in payment. In March 1868, he set out in the middle of a fierce blizzard. Between Toronto and Montreal the train bogged down in huge snowdrifts and didn't turn a wheel for twenty-four hours. The passengers had to be taken out on snowshoes. The train arrived in Boston four days late.

When Tom applied for a job at Western Union, everybody roared with laughter. He had on his wide-brimmed hat, baggy old clothes and the duster, in which he had been sleeping for a week. He was chewing tobacco. But when the ragged country hick sat down at the telegraph key, he was hired in five minutes.

Edison was assigned to the number one wire to receive press copy for the *Boston Herald*. The other operators in the office planned this as a joke, knowing that the fastest sender in New York was on the other end of the wire. They had arranged with the sender to start slowly and work up to top speed and then to slur words and mix signals. Tom took the copy as fast as the man could send it and had time to stop now and then to calmly sharpen his pencil. Finally he tapped out a message to the New Yorker: "Hey, young man, change off and send with the other foot!"

After that, nobody laughed at Tom Edison in that office.

4

Practical Inventor

One of the most pleasant interludes in Tom Edison's young life was spent in Boston. He and Milt Adams shared a place at a rooming house and took their meals at a boarding house about a mile away. G. F. Milliken, the manager of the Boston telegraph service, was fond of Tom and seemed to realize that he was unusual. This made him more patient with his employee's practical jokes. For instance, he didn't fire Tom when the young man wired the dipper in the water bucket, so that everybody who took a drink of water got an electric shock.

Boston was a wonderful place to be. To begin with there was the Boston Public Library. And the northern part of the city, with its quaint old buildings and winding streets, thrilled the boy from Michigan. He and Milt wandered among the second-hand bookshops and junk stores in old Boston. One day Tom bought second-hand a two-volume work by Michael Faraday, *Experimental Researches in Electricity*. These books opened up a whole new world to him.

Faraday, an English scientist who had recently died, was one of Tom Edison's greatest heroes. Faraday had been a poor boy who, like Tom, had never gone to school. Early in life he was apprenticed to a bookbinder, where he learned many things he was able to use later in his life. At the age of twenty-two, Faraday became assistant to Sir Humphry Davy at the Royal Institute in London. He made many marvelous discoveries, but probably the most important was the dynamo —a large magnet with a disk rotating between its poles—which demonstrated how mechanical energy could be made into electrical energy.

Faraday was an unselfish man who never seemed to care for money or titles. He loved truth and was always humble before the wonders of nature that he discovered. His writings were simple, and he explained his ideas and inventions without the use of complicated mathematical formulas.

Edison brought his treasured books home at three o'clock in the morning and started to read. When Milt Adams awoke, Tom was still at it, and was wildly excited.

"Adams, I'm already twenty-one years old," Tom said. "I've got so much to do, and life is so short, that I'm going to hustle." With that he started on a dead run for the boarding house to eat breakfast.

In Boston, Edison experimented whenever he was not at work. When he was at work, he spent any time he could spare from the telegraph key dreaming and drawing his diagrams. His room was, as ever, a library-laboratory and it was almost impossible to find a place to sit down in it, much less sleep.

He had read about Alfred Nobel's dynamite and he decided to experiment with that. He and Milt concocted some nitroglycerin and combined it with inert matter, producing an explosion that scared them both half to death.

"It dawned on us we had a very large white elephant in our possession," Edison later said. "At 6 a.m. I put the explosive in a sarsaparilla bottle, tied a string to it, wrapped it in paper and put it gently into a sewer at the corner of State and Washington Streets!"

Tom experimented with everything. He was still working on a telegraph that would send two messages at the same time. He knew that if he could find a way to send more than one message on the same wire at the same time, telegraphy would become cheap enough for everybody to use.

Milton Adams wrote an article about Tom's experiments. It was printed in *The Journal of the Telegraph*. The attention this story received gave Edison the idea of quitting his job with Western Union to become an inventor. Sending and receiving messages bored him, and tempted him to play jokes on his boss. One day he copied the stock-market quotations he was receiving in such small handwriting that they could not be read without a magnifying glass. When the manager complained, Edison copied the quotations in such large handwriting that only a few letters appeared on a page and resulted in a bundle of pages too heavy to carry. He was demoted.

In January 1869, he resigned and became a free-lance inventor. He had made friends with Charles Williams, Jr., who had a machine shop at 109 Court Street. Tom set up shop in one corner of Williams' place of business. He had no regular income. There was nothing new to Tom about being poor. Still, he had to have money to get his inventions started. He persuaded one man in Boston to advance him five hundred dollars for a share in the future profits of his double-message telegraph. He got a hundred dollars from another man for a machine he was working on to record votes.

On June 1, 1869, Tom Edison received his first patent from the United States Patent Office, for the vote-recording machine. Tom got the idea for this machine as a Western Union telegraph receiver, when he reported the oral votes of congressmen and senators and noticed how slow the process was. Edison whittled the first model of this machine out of wood. In his machine, wires with switches were attached to the seats of persons in the voting chamber of the legislature. The lawmakers could register their votes instantly on a telegraphic instrument through electric impulse. A revolution of the cylinder printed the voter's name in the proper column, and the votes were totaled automatically on a dial.

Tom expected his vote recorder to be an instant success. One of his friends took the machine proudly to the Massachusetts legislature. But he brought it back again.

"It's a failure, Tom," he said.

"Impossible," Tom cried. "I *know* it will work."

"That's the trouble," his friend said. "It *does* work. But with this machine there can be no filibuster, which legislators consider necessary. They wouldn't give it house room!"

Tom was downcast. "Ever after," he said, "I

looked out for the need of any particular invention before I attempted to reduce it to practice. To this decision I have made it the rule of my life to adhere."

The vote-recording machine, his first patent, was a failure because nobody wanted it. This

A model of the vote recorder, Edison's first patented invention and ancestor of the modern voting machine

experience turned Tom Edison into a practical inventor. Although the invention did not sell, it did attract attention. Tom Edison began to be regarded as a real inventor in Boston.

He was invited by a Boston academy to lecture on telegraphy to its students. But on the day he was to give his speech, he forgot all about it. He was up on the roof stringing a telegraph wire when Milt came running up to remind him. It was then so late Edison left for the school in his work clothes without combing his cowlicked hair. When he got to the academy he found, to his horror, that his class was composed of elegant young ladies. It had never occurred to him that the audience wouldn't be boys. His tongue went dry and he thought for a moment he would have to run. But he pulled himself together and told his audience whatever he could think of about telegraphy and electricity. The girls applauded heartily. Whenever they saw Tom after that, they bowed and smiled and gave every indication of wanting to know him better. He was too shy to follow their lead.

Tom usually had several experiments going at the same time. While he was in Boston, he began to work on an improved stock-quotation printing machine, on which the changes in the prices of stocks in Wall Street could be registered automatically.

And he returned to his old dream of a machine

that would permit the sending of more than one telegraph message at a time. The growing importance of telegraphy made other inventors interested in this problem, and Edison feared someone would beat him to the solution. One of the inventors who was working on the duplex telegraph was J. B. Stearns, who also lived in Boston.

When Edison had made sufficient progress, he asked permission to rearrange the offices of Western Union in Boston according to his own system. Western Union refused. Edison then offered his machine to Western Union's rival, the Atlantic & Pacific Telegraph Company. He was given permission to try his invention over the wire between Rochester, N. Y., and New York City.

Edison borrowed eight hundred dollars and left for Rochester, carrying all his machinery in his baggage. He set up his equipment in Rochester, but he never got any response from New York. Although the telegrapher there had been briefed, he did not really understand how the invention worked and couldn't carry out his part. The trial ended in failure. The work of months and the dreaming of years were wiped out, along with all the money Edison had earned and all he had borrowed. Returning to Boston, he found he could no longer borrow money there. He decided to move to New York.

Thomas Edison reached the sidewalks of New

York in the dawn of a spring morning without a cent in his pocket. He was also very hungry. He stared in bewilderment at the tangle of horse cars, wagons, carriages and carts in the roaring streets. As he walked past Washington Market, he saw a man tasting tea in one of the wholesale houses that lined the wharf. Edison went in and asked for a sample of the tea, so that he could taste it. Flattered, the man gave him a little packet of fine tea.

Tom took his prize to the first restaurant he came to and offered to swap it for something to eat. Impressed with the quality of the tea, the restaurant man traded Tom an apple dumpling and a cup of coffee for it. Forever after, Tom Edison's favorite food was apple dumpling. It was a good thing he liked it because he lived on it for some time.

Edison had no place to sleep, so he walked the streets all night long. He finally located a telegrapher he had known in his tramp days, but the man was also out of work. He could lend Tom only one dollar. Apple dumpling and coffee cost five cents, and Tom figured he could make the dollar last several days if he stuck to that menu. He wandered around the city for several days living on five-cent meals.

Tom finally decided to call on Franklin Pope, an electrical engineer and telegraph expert who worked as superintendent of the Gold Indicator

Company in the financial district. Pope had heard of Tom Edison and his Boston inventions. He had no job for him, but he offered Tom a cot in the cellar of the Gold Indicator Company. Glad for any roof over his head, Edison slept in a cellar and lived on his apple dumplings in the heart of the financial district, where millions of dollars were changing hands every day all around him.

The Gold Indicator Company depended on the Laws transmitter. It had been invented by Dr. Samuel S. Laws, Pope's boss. It was a telegraphic instrument that operated an electrical indicator and registered price changes on a big board in the Gold Room of the Stock Exchange. This machine sent changes in gold prices by wire to the offices of more than three hundred stockbrokers, who paid high fees for the service.

In that summer of 1869, gambling in gold was at a fever pitch. One day when excitement in the gold market was running high, the whole central transmitting system of the Gold Indicator Company's machinery ground to a halt. Pope rushed into the shop to find out what the trouble was. Dr. Laws came running out of his office. Neither of them could find out what was wrong. When the instruments in the brokers' offices stopped registering, the brokers began to send messengers on foot to find out what had happened. In a few minutes a mob of several hundred people pushed into the Gold Indicator Company's offices. Pope was too excited and nervous to handle the machinery. Laws began to shout and scream and try to drive people out of the building. He saw his successful business being wiped out.

Tom walked over to the machine and noticed that one of the springs had dropped off between two gear wheels. He struggled through the crowd to Laws and Pope, who were now yelling at each other.

"I think I know where the trouble is," Tom called out above the hubbub.

"Fix it! Fix it!" yelled Laws. "Hurry!"

Tom removed the broken spring, put in a new one and reset the dials. He also sent linemen to all the brokers' offices to adjust their receivers. In two hours, the Gold Indicator was back in business.

When Laws recovered from his tantrum, he sent for Tom Edison. He hired Tom at a salary far larger than anything he had ever been paid, to act as assistant to Franklin Pope. A couple of months later, Pope resigned to go into business for himself. Tom succeeded Pope as electrical engineer for the Gold Indicator Company, at the fabulous salary of three hundred dollars per month. Edison improved the Laws instruments. Not long after, the company was bought by Western Union. Tom decided he didn't want to work for Western Union. So once more he was unemployed.

Edison and Pope remained friends. In October 1869 they formed their own firm called Pope, Edison & Company, Electrical Engineers. They had another partner named J. H. Ashley. This was the first professional electrical engineering service in the United States. Franklin Pope was still in his twenties, and Thomas Edison was twenty-two. To save money, Tom boarded with Pope and his wife in Elizabeth, New Jersey. He commuted to Jersey City, where the new firm had rented an old shop near the Pennsylvania Railroad yards. Tom worked from 6 a.m. to 1 a.m.

One of the first machines Edison perfected was an improved stock printer, which was soon bought up by Western Union to remove it from competition. The engineering firm received fifteen thousand dollars, of which Edison's share was five thousand. To Edison, it seemed more money than he had ever hoped to have.

Tom soon tangled with his partners. He felt he was doing all the work. He left the firm and struck out on his own. He had begun to realize the importance of his work to Western Union and its branch company, the Gold & Stock Telegraph Company, headed by General Marshall Lefferts. Edison had submitted a number of his inventions and improvements on existing equipment to Western Union, and several had been adopted.

One day, before a group of engineers in General Lefferts' office, Thomas Edison demon-

69

strated a device he had invented which would control errors in stock tickers. The engineers were impressed.

The Universal Printer, a stock ticker invented by Edison for the Gold & Stock Telegraph Company

"Well, young fellow, how much do you think your improvements are worth?" Lefferts said to him. "Let's settle up our bill."

Edison thought his inventions and improvements were worth at least five thousand dollars, but he was ready to settle for three thousand.

"I don't know," Edison said. "Make me an offer."

"How would forty thousand dollars strike you?" General Lefferts asked.

Tom nearly fainted but pulled himself together and accepted. In later years he enjoyed relating what happened next.

He was told to return in two days for the contract and his money. When he got over his excitement, he began to feel sure that it was all a trick—one of those Wall Street tricks he had heard about. He decided that if he ever got a cent he would be lucky.

He went back to Lefferts' office and signed the contract. He was given a check, the first one he had ever received. He took it to the bank it was drawn on. He had never been in a bank, so he hung around outside, watching the people stand in line and move up to the tellers' windows. Finally he entered and got in line. When he reached the window and handed in his check, the teller began to shout at him. Tom couldn't understand a word because of his deafness. He took his check back and sadly dropped out of line.

So it was a trick after all, he thought, almost in tears, as he sat dismally on the steps of the bank. But he returned to Lefferts' office, where he spoke to a clerk. The clerk said that the teller had only wanted Edison to endorse the check and to be identified. The clerk took Tom back to the bank and identified him. The teller then handed Tom forty thousand dollars in ten- and twenty-dollar bills.

Thirty days later, Edison had spent the entire amount on his first shop and its equipment and was again without money. He rented the third floor of a dingy building at 4-6 Ward Street, in Newark, New Jersey, and began to install his machinery and advertise for mechanics in the newspapers. For he had an order for twelve hundred of his new stock tickers from Western Union. And he was under contract to concede to Western Union an option on all of his telegraphic inventions.

Although Tom Edison was shrewd in many ways, he had little interest in the business side of his business. "I kept only payroll accounts," he said later. "I kept no books. I preserved a record of my own expenditures on one hook, and the bills on another hook, and generally gave notes in payment. The first intimation that a note was due was the protest; after that I had to hustle around and raise the money. This saved the humbuggery of bookkeeping which I never understood."

72

Tom had peculiar ideas about work, and there were no set working hours in his shop. His employees were inspired by his excitement and enthusiasm and did not know when to quit work any more than he did. Nobody worked *for* Edison; they worked *with* him. He worked side by side with the youngest mechanic, and there was no chore that he would not and did not do. His assistants were like brothers, and his companionship and leadership made them a part of all his brilliant ideas. Nothing in the world was more exciting than their work.

Edison took another partner in his manufacturing firm—William Unger—and the company of Edison & Unger began to hire men to manufacture the stock tickers. The electrical industry was at its very beginning, and most of the men who were interested in making electrical equipment were clockmakers or machinists. Their wages were just average, and they were all perfectionists. When Edison had something important to finish, he would bribe them with sums of money or lay bets that they couldn't do it in the time allowed. This made them work all the harder. When they had finished a hard job, he sometimes had a party right in the laboratory. Or he would close the shop and take everybody on a fishing trip.

Once when Edison had a rush order for stock printers worth thirty thousand dollars, and the

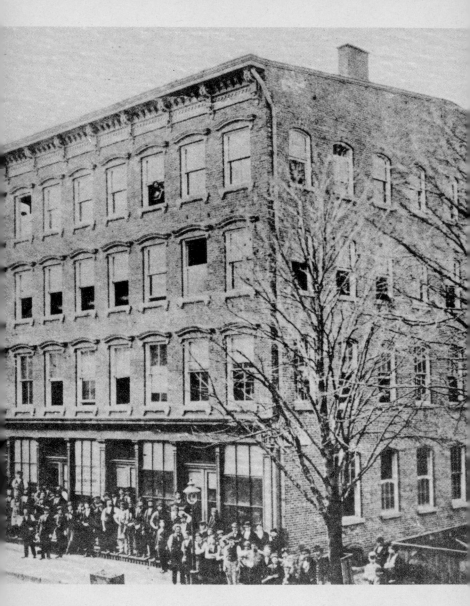

74

machines developed trouble, he called his men together and said: "Now, you fellows, I've locked the door and you'll have to stay here until we find the cause of this trouble."

For sixty hours they worked, with little food and less sleep, while their wives stood outside and complained and cried, or tried to push packages of food through the windows of their prison. But Edison would not give in. Not until the job was finished would he unlock the door. Nobody held this against him—with the possible exception of the wives. When the work was finished, they all had a big celebration.

Edison at this time was a smooth-shaven man of twenty-four, with the same broad brow, big head, pale blue eyes and unruly hair of his childhood. Most of his employees were years older than he was, but they called him the Old Man.

The five years he spent in Newark were satisfying ones for Edison. He installed a small private laboratory where he spent some time every day on his research and experiments. His reputation made other inventors seek him out, and he was always engaged in getting "the bugs" out of new machines. His mind was busy with new inventions. While he was a practical inven-

The Newark factory in 1873

tor, he wasn't always a very practical person.

One day he received a notice that if he didn't pay his taxes the next day, he would have to pay interest of 12½ percent and a penalty. He went to the city hall to stand in line. While he stood there, his mind roved over the problem of the multiple telegraph sender. When he got up to the window, the tax collector said: "All right, young man, what is your name?"

Edison looked up in surprise.

"I don't know, sir," he stammered.

"Then I can't help you," the man said, and waved him aside.

The line moved up and Edison still couldn't think of his name. The hour struck, the day of grace was over and he had to pay 12½ percent extra. He had to ask a man he recognized in the street what his own name was.

5

Deaf Sound Man

Although Tom Edison had earned enough money in Newark to buy a frock coat and a stovepipe hat, he had no real home. He was still a bachelor, living in a furnished room. His deafness made him timid about girls.

According to family tradition, one night when he was coming out of his shop in a rainstorm he found two young ladies standing in the doorway trying to keep from getting wet. He invited them to come inside the shop out of the rain. He could not keep from staring at the beauty of the younger girl, who wore her blond hair in a high pompadour. He could not get her out of his mind later, so he made it his business to find out who she was. Her name was Mary Stilwell and she was just sixteen years old. She and her sister, Alice, who came from a genteel family with very little money, were Sunday-school teachers.

Tom Edison offered Mary Stilwell a job, punching perforations in telegraph tape. It was not usual for ladies to work outside their homes in those days, but Edison had several women working in his shop. Miss Stilwell decided to take the job.

Tom's courtship was like everything else about him—different. At first he just stood in the shop and stared at Mary Stilwell. She never raised her eyes from her work until his prolonged stare began to make her nervous. "Oh, Mr. Edison," she would cry then and drop her hands in her lap.

Edison always had to move closer in order to hear. One day he said: "What do you think of me, little girl? Do you like me?"

"Oh, Mr. Edison, you frighten me!" Miss Stilwell answered.

"Don't be in a hurry about telling me," Tom said. "It doesn't matter much, unless you'd like to marry me. Think it over, talk to your mother and

Mary Stilwell Edison soon after her marriage

78

let me know . . . next week, Tuesday, I mean."

The next week Mary Stilwell gave Tom Edison permission to call on her. In those days, young couples were chaperoned. But Tom's deafness made the whispers and sighs associated with courtship impossible. He hit on a splendid idea. He taught Mary the Morse code, so that he could talk to her by tapping a silver quarter in the palm of her hand. This enabled Tom to talk more freely to Mary in the presence of her parents.

One day, when they were sitting in her parents' parlor, he tapped out: "I have been thinking of you all the time. Would you marry me?"

Miss Stilwell reached for the coin and tapped out in his palm: "That would make me very happy."

That was how Edison became engaged.

Tom Edison and Mary Stilwell were married on Christmas Day, 1871. Edison's mother had died in April, and there were no members of his family at the wedding. After the wedding breakfast, Tom took his bride to the new house he had bought at 97 Wright Street in Newark. As soon as they got there and were alone at last, Tom began to worry about some stock tickers he was working on. He told his bride that he thought he would have to go down to the factory for a while. The new Mrs. Edison did not want to cross him, and an hour after the ceremony the groom rushed off to his shop.

Mary spent her wedding day alone, frightened and in tears. Late at night Joseph Murray, one of Tom's friends and co-workers, dropped into the shop.

"What are you doing here, Tom?" he shouted at Edison.

"What time is it?" Edison asked.

"It's midnight," Murray said.

"I must go home," Tom said. "I got married today!"

The next day Tom and Mary left for Niagara Falls for a honeymoon. The bride was so upset that she insisted on taking her sister, Alice.

Mary was a sweet, gentle woman, and she tried to make a home for Tom. But he was not like other husbands. He always had his mind on his work and sometimes forgot to come home at all. In spite of having worked in the shop, Mary Edison did not understand Tom's inventions, even when he tried to explain them to her. But she never complained. She admired her husband and forgave him everything.

About this time, Edison at last perfected his invention which made it possible to send several messages at the same time on one telegraph wire. J. B. Stearns had already patented a duplex telegraph, but Edison's invention was an improvement—a quadruplex, sending two messages in each direction at the same time.

There was still great competition between Western Union and the rival company headed by Jay Gould, the Atlantic & Pacific Telegraph Company. Edison, as a free-lance inventor, was willing to work for any company. He offered his quadruplex telegraph invention to Western Union. He was unable to sell it until he made an arrangement with George B. Prescott, chief engineer of Western Union, to use Prescott's name and give him a share of the profits. This deal made it possible for Edison to use the equipment of Western Union to perfect his invention.

Edison was in debt and badly needed money. While he had used Western Union's facilities and personnel, he had received no payments from them. When Jay Gould offered to buy Edison's remaining share of the quadruplex invention for thirty thousand dollars, Edison agreed. Then began the great telegraphic war between Western Union and the Atlantic & Pacific Telegraph Company. Edison was accused of being a traitor to Western Union. Western Union sued to have Edison's assignment of patent rights to Gould's company canceled. The court trials were unpleasant for Edison.

In 1875 Gould began to merge all the telegraph

companies under his control. Edison was promised payment in stock amounting to $250,000 and named chief electrician of the merged companies at a good salary. Edison soon found that Gould did not keep his promises. Tom was defrauded of the money and did not get the job. Gould eventually obtained control of Western Union, and he ruled over it until he died.

"When Gould got the Western Union," Edison wrote later, "I knew no further progress in telegraphy was possible, and I went into other lines."

After this trouble, some of his shops had to shut down and Edison had to borrow money to save his home. He was very disillusioned.

Tom decided to give up his manufacturing business in Newark and move to a lonely spot in the country. There he would do nothing but invent new things. He bought a piece of land in Menlo Park, in Middlesex County, New Jersey, between Elizabeth and Metuchen, on the Pennsylvania Railroad. Menlo Park had only a half-dozen houses. In an open pasture, Tom built a two-story wooden building a hundred feet long and twenty-five feet wide, with a porch in front and a picket fence to keep out the cows.

On the first floor he had his office, a library for books and a drafting room. The second floor was one long, barnlike laboratory with all his equipment and desks for thirteen mechanics. Edison

A drawing of the world's first industrial laboratory, in Menlo Park, New Jersey. The electric railway which Edison developed in later years is in the upper right.

sat at a table. This was the first industrial research laboratory in the world.

Tom bought a farmhouse nearby for his family. Most of his men stayed at Mrs. Jordan's Boarding House, the only boarding place in the village. There was really nothing to do in Menlo Park but invent things.

On January 14, 1876, Edison filed with the United States Patent Office a document called a *caveat,* giving formal notice that he was working on a telephone.

The telephone had something in common with the telegraph, which transmitted letters and numbers in code over a wire. But the telephone was designed to reproduce the actual sound of the human voice, transmitted over a wire. The first electrical telephone had been described by a German inventor named Johann Philipp Reis, in 1861.

Other experimenters who were working on the telephone were Alexander Graham Bell of Salem, Massachusetts, and Elisha Gray of Chicago. When Bell was experimenting with his instrument, he went to Western Union, hoping to be able to make use of their wires for testing. He discovered that Gray had already patented a harmonic telegraph to transmit musical sounds and had assigned it to Western Union. After that, Bell worked in secrecy on his telephone.

Although it was still incomplete, Edison was also experimenting with an instrument that would carry the sound of the human voice over wires.

Exactly one month after Edison's application was filed, Bell filed his application for a patent on a completed telephone. On the same day, Elisha Gray filed a caveat. Both these inventors had finished models of an instrument capable of carrying sounds. On March 7, Bell was awarded the patent. Three days later, the sound of a human voice was first transmitted over the Bell telephone.

Bell's invention was at first looked on largely as a curiosity. The principle of the machine was the generation of a weak electric current by the vibration of a diaphragm—a thin circular plate—against an electromagnet. The same instrument was used for both talking and listening. The person talking spoke into the instrument, while the person listening put a similar instrument against his ear. When the person who was listening decided to talk, the instrument was reversed at both ends of the line. However, the sound was very weak and the machine was not considered very practical.

When Bell offered to sell it to Western Union for $100,000, his offer was refused. Bell finally managed to finance the Bell Telephone Company himself and started to manufacture telephones. They soon found favor with businessmen, who began to use them instead of the telegraph.

Western Union decided to get into the telephone business. William Orton, then president of

The Edison telephone, unlike Bell's instrument, had a separate transmitter and receiver.

the company, asked Edison if he could improve on Bell's phone. Orton offered to pay Edison $150 a week for five years to work on it. Edison accepted.

The transmitter-receiver of Bell's telephone was constructed of a diaphragm of soft iron, placed close to the pole of a magnet on which was wound a coil of fine wire.

Edison wanted to find a material that would convert the sound of the voice into electrical currents more clearly. He tried everything—sponges, moist paper, felt, graphite, quicksilver, cork, lead and mercury. He invented fifty different telephones and while the sound improved and grew clearer with each one, he wasn't satisfied. One night when he was working late in his laboratory, his kerosene lamp went out. When he went to put more oil in it, he happened to notice that the lamp chimney was blackened. He scraped off the carbon black and applied it to the disk in the telephone receiver. The volume of sound immediately became much stronger.

Edison's improved transmitter included a battery whose power was used to produce a current in a local circuit. It was possible to vary the current by pressure of the vibrating diaphragm on the carbon button in the circuit. Edison's developments made the telephone more practical, and the carbon transmitter he invented is still in use on every telephone.

Tom was also responsible for the way we answer the telephone today. Originally people wound the phone with a crank, which rang a bell, and then said: "Are you there?" This took too much time for Edison. During one of the hundreds of tests made in his laboratory, he picked up the phone one day, twisted the crank and shouted: "Hello!" This became the way to answer the telephone all over America, and it still is.

Edison received $100,000 for his improvements on the telephone. A telephone war then started when the Bell Telephone Company modified and adapted some of Edison's improvements, which Western Union claimed. Finally, the Western Union Company agreed to get out of the telephone business for a 20 percent royalty on the Bell Telephone Company's future earnings. (As part of the agreement, the Bell Telephone Company got out of the telegraph business.)

Thus, many millions of dollars were earned for Western Union by Edison's work on the telephone. By paying the royalty, the Bell Telephone Company was able to make use of all Edison's improvements, including the carbon transmitter, so that this company profited also. Edison received only his salary for the work.

Edison was always looking for ideas and was keenly aware of little things. While he was experimenting with the telephone, something happened that interested him. "I was singing to the mouth-piece of a telephone," he said, "when the vibrations of my voice sent the fine steel point into my finger. That set me thinking. If I could record the actions of the point, and send the point over the same surface afterward, I saw no reason why the thing would not talk. I tried the experiment first on a strip of telegraph paper, and found that the point made an alphabet. I shouted the words: 'Halloo! Halloo!' into the mouth-piece, ran the paper over the steel point, and heard a faint 'Halloo! Halloo!' in return. The phonograph is the result of the pricking of a finger."

Edison made a drawing of a roller with grooves around it. At each side of the roller was a short metal tube with a diaphragm. A needle stuck out from the center of each diaphragm. The roller had a crank handle for turning it.

He gave this drawing to an associate, John Kruesi, and asked him to make a model of it. Kruesi asked what it was.

"It's going to be a machine that talks," Edison said, "just like you and me."

Edison said he was thinking about the telegraph repeater and the telephone, and he believed it would be possible to make a machine that would record the sound of the human voice

Two sketches of a phonograph, from Edison's notebook

Phonograph.

Nov 29th 1877

Chas Batc

and play it back. In short, a phonograph.

"But no metal will be affected by sound waves," Kruesi said. "It would take some voice to leave an impression on metal!"

"No, but I think tinfoil or paraffin paper might," Edison said. "We will wrap tinfoil around the cylinder. I will speak through the tube. Then I will turn the crank and make the cylinder go around and the diaphragm will vibrate under the needle. The machine will repeat what I say."

The men in the shop all shook their heads. The Old Man (who was only thirty years old) was losing his mind.

"Just make the model," Edison instructed, "and don't be faint-hearted."

Kruesi set to work. He worked all night as usual. At dawn his wife arrived as usual with a pot of coffee and some buns and the usual complaints. Bleary-eyed, Kruesi drank his coffee and went back to work. At the end of thirty hours, he brought the model to Edison.

"Now go home and get some sleep," Edison told him.

"If that thing can talk I want to hear it!" Kruesi said.

Edison put his arm around Kruesi's shoulder. "All right," he said. "Somebody bring me some tinfoil."

Everybody in the laboratory crowded around the model and Edison began to apply a sheet of tinfoil to the grooved cylinder. At first the foil tore, but finally Edison glued the ends together to hold it taut. He turned the crank and the cylinder revolved. Edison spoke into one of the tubes: "Mary had a little lamb, its fleece was white as snow, and everywhere that Mary went, the lamb was sure to go. . . ."

When he had finished the rhyme, he turned the roller back to the starting point, put the second diaphragm needle into position and started turning the crank again. Faint and far away, but distinctly in Edison's voice, they now heard the poem repeated.

It was a moment of terrible awe—a miracle.

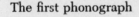

The first phonograph

John Kruesi, weakened by lack of sleep, almost fell over in a faint.

"Here, Kruesi, you say something to it," Edison said.

Kruesi said something in German.

The same thing happened.

Then the silence broke and there was wild jubilation. Everybody wanted to try it. The rest of the night they talked, sang and whistled at the cylinder and heard themselves repeated by the inanimate machine.

Edison sent everybody home to bed, but he didn't feel sleepy. He kept on tinkering with his new toy.

Then he put the model under his arm, caught the train for New York and went to the office of Alfred Ely Beach, the editor of the *Scientific American.*

"Well, Mr. Edison, what have you got there?" Beach asked.

Tom Edison grinned. "Turn this crank and you'll find out," he said.

Beach turned the crank suspiciously.

"Good morning, Mr. Beach," the machine said in Edison's voice. "What do you think of the phonograph?"

For us today it is almost impossible to realize the excitement that people felt when they heard a machine talk for the first time. News of the miracle spread through the building, and people began to crowd into the office. Excited reporters arrived from all the newspapers. The office became so jammed that it was feared the floor would collapse, and Beach persuaded Edison to take the machine away.

The whole world was stunned to read in the papers the next morning that Tom Edison had invented a talking machine. Thousands of people decided to descend on Menlo Park. The Pennsylvania Railroad had to run special excursion trains to take care of the crowd.

A telegram arrived for Edison from Washington, asking him to demonstrate the talking machine. Edison went to Washington on April 18, 1878, with the phonograph tucked under his arm and played it for congressmen and scientists. They were amazed. He was summoned to the White House by President Rutherford B. Hayes at 11:00 p.m. Mrs. Hayes hastily got out of bed, and the President and his wife and Carl Schurz, the Secretary of the Interior, kept Edison at the Executive Mansion until 4:00 a.m., playing the phonograph.

Edison was as overwhelmed by this invention as everybody else. He played with it as if it were a toy. Edison was now the father of a four-year-old child—a girl named Marion Estelle, whom he nicknamed Dot after the Morse code.

He decided to record his daughter's voice and tried to make her cry. Dot was an amiable child

and he couldn't get her to cry for the phonograph. He tumbled her around and made faces at her and pulled her hair but she simply stared at him. Losing patience, Edison bared the child's leg and was about to pinch or bite it, when his wife caught him in the act.

"Thomas Edison!" Mary cried. "What are you doing?"

"I wanted to make a recording of a child's cry," Edison said sheepishly.

"Aren't you ashamed," Mary said and picked up the little girl.

Several weeks later, Mary Edison brought Marion to the laboratory to see her father. The noise of the machinery frightened the child, and made her burst into tears and wail loudly.

"Stop the machinery," Edison shouted, "and start the phonograph!"

So he got his wish in the end.

Edison received a patent for the phonograph on February 19, 1878. The files of the United States Patent Office showed that no other attempt had ever been made to record the human voice.

Many years and millions of dollars went into

Charles Batchelor (left) and Edison with the phonograph Edison demonstrated in Washington, D.C. This photograph was taken in the studio of the famous Civil War photographer Mathew Brady.

the perfecting of the phonograph. Edison soon decided that tinfoil was unsatisfactory and began to experiment with wax. He finally settled on stearin, an animal fat used in making soap, from which he produced an almost indestructible cylinder with a surface so smooth that there was no rasping or scratching from the needle. For ten years Edison did no further work on the phonograph, which soon became merely a curiosity. This was a mistake that cost him a great deal in the end.

The talking machine achieved great popularity with crowned heads. Queen Victoria of Great Britain, Czar Alexander of Russia, Kaiser Wilhelm of Germany and even the Dalai Lama of Tibet recorded their voices on it. It eventually became a source of education, pleasure and entertainment, and people still love it.

In a magazine article, Edison prophesied that the phonograph would have the following uses:

Letter writing and all kinds of dictation without the aid of a stenographer.

Phonographic books, which would speak to blind people without effort on their part.

The teaching of elocution.

Music. The phonograph will undoubtedly be liberally devoted to music.

The family record; preserving the sayings, the voices, the last words of the dying members of the family, as of great men.

Music boxes, toys etc. A doll which may speak, sing, cry or laugh may be promised our children for the Christmas holidays ensuing.

Clocks, that should announce in speech the hour of the day, call you home to lunch, send your lover home at ten, etc.

The preservation of language by reproduction of our Washingtons, our Lincolns, our Gladstones.

Educational purposes; such as preserving the instructions of a teacher so that the pupil can refer to them at any moment; or learn spelling lessons.

The perfection or advancement of the telephone's art by the phonograph, making that instrument an auxiliary in the transmission of permanent records.

Many of these predictions have come true. Although Edison abandoned the phonograph for a decade, it brought him his first public fame.

6

Lighter of the Lamp

Edison's years at Menlo Park were rewarding. His family grew. A son, Thomas A. Edison, Jr., came along to keep Dot company. Edison nicknamed his son Dash. Then another son, William Leslie, was born.

Edison was an unusual father. He loved his children but he could not keep from teasing them. When he stayed home on Sundays to be with his wife and family, he would play wild, rough games with the children or play tricks on them, so they often wound up in tears. But when he was working on an invention, he forgot everything else. His mind was far away and he paid no attention to his children. It was hard for them to understand him.

Edison had never had a vacation. He did not know what the word meant. But after all the excitement about the phonograph and the crowds of people who came to Menlo Park to look at him and his inventions, he began to feel very tired. He was now famous, and he received many invitations to go places and do things. When Professor George Barker invited him to come to the Rocky Mountains in July 1878 to watch a total eclipse of the sun, he decided to go. The party was a group of scientists and astronomers from Pennsylvania, Princeton, and Columbia universities. Edison had invented an instrument called a micro-tasimeter (MY-crow-tuh-SIM-uh-tur) to measure slight changes in temperature, and he wanted to try it out in the mountains.

On the day of the eclipse, July 29, Edison set up his tasimeter near a henhouse on the side of a mountain. When the sun's eclipse made it dark in the daytime, the chickens all came home to roost; so Edison had some unwelcome company. Then a storm came up and the henhouse began to blow away. Edison held on to a telescope and tried to keep his other instruments from blowing off the mountain while the chickens ran around, clucking wildly. His micro-tasimeter was so sensitive

Edison and other scientists preparing to watch the solar eclipse at Rawlins, Wyoming, in 1878. Edison is second from right.

that the heat of the sun's corona drove the needle right off the scale.

But Edison enjoyed talking to the other scientists, and after the eclipse he went off on a hunting trip with them. He then decided to go

with Professor Barker to California to get a look at
the rest of the country. They rode on the Union
Pacific Railroad, on which Edison had a lifetime
pass, extended as a courtesy to the famous inventor. Of course, Edison loved trains, and this trip
reminded him of his boyhood. He had always
wanted to ride on the cowcatcher of an engine.
He asked the officials of the Union Pacific if he
could ride on the cowcatcher of their train.

Edison was such a celebrity now that any wish
he made was granted. The engineers gave him a
sofa cushion and he sat on the prow of the engine.
He rode from Omaha, Nebraska, to Sacramento,
California, on the prow of the train with nothing
to obscure his view. The other members of the
party were sure he would be thrown off and
killed. Edison insisted on his perch, even after
the train hit a bear and the bear's body missed
him by inches as the locomotive hurtled on.
Edison got in the cab of the engine only when the
intense cold on top of the Sierra Nevada Mountains drove him inside, or when the train came to
a tunnel.

On the way home, Professor Barker and Edison stopped off at Yosemite. While there, they
watched miners drilling and boring iron ore by
hand.

"Barky," Tom said to the professor, "that work
would be easier if we could harness Yosemite's
falls and turn the power into electricity."

"Work would be easier for miners and everybody else," Barky said. "But it's not likely."

"Someday our great waterfalls will make electric power enough to light every home and factory in the world," Edison prophesied, "and we won't have to bother with gas lamps anymore."

"You ought to meet Bill Wallace, a friend of mine," Barky said. "He's trying to make an electric lamp."

Edison was very much interested. "Let's go!" he said.

Soon after Edison's return to Menlo Park, he went to Ansonia, Connecticut, where Wallace was working on a version of the arc light. The arc light was a luminous electric glow, shaped like a bow, produced under certain conditions when a break was made in an electric circuit. The first arc light had been produced by the British scientist Sir Humphry Davy many years before. A Russian engineer named Jablochkoff had improved it. The trouble with the arc light was that it gave off a harsh light and tremendous heat and would burn only a few hours.

At this time people outside of big cities lighted their homes, worked and lived by oil lamps or candlelight. In the city, gas lights were generally used. Streets were lit by gas lights, as were places of business and theaters. Some home owners were using gas lighting, but it was expensive and not always satisfactory. The gas lights were smelly and unpleasant. And there was no general system of distribution. People who used gas lights had to put in their own systems.

Edison wanted to improve the quality of illumination. He wanted not a blinding light, like the arc light, but a mild light, like that of gas lighting—without its drawbacks. He foresaw a widespread electrical system, serving people everywhere.

Edison was excited when he saw Wallace's laboratory. "But I think you are going about it wrong," Edison said to Wallace. "I believe that to chain electric current we will have to divide it, so the light won't be so hot and blinding."

"Divide electric current!" Wallace scoffed. "Why, that's impossible."

"I believe it can be done," Edison said. From then on he couldn't wait to get back to his own laboratory.

The electric light caused Edison the most work and trouble of all his inventions. He said that he tried out 3,000 different theories while he was working on the electric light.

"I was never discouraged," Edison said, "but I cannot say the same for other people who were working with me."

He predicted that within two years he would subdivide electric current and invent a lamp that would turn night into day. Also he declared he would find a way to convert the power of steam into electricity, so that a few steam plants, turning dynamos, could produce electric current to light every house and shop and factory in a city. Some newspapers called him a boaster and a fool.

Tom did not have time to read the newspapers just then, and he paid no attention to what other people said anyway. He planned to start manufacturing electric lamps as soon as he perfected his invention.

Edison wanted to find a filament that would heat up enough to give off light, without melting or burning up. First he made strips of carbonized paper, but he decided they were too easily destroyed. He then made fine threads of rare metals—barium, rhodium, ruthenium, titanium, zirconium and platinum. Platinum seemed to be best. He wound a double spiral of fine platinum wire and put it in a glass tube. He then invented a regulator which he attached to the lamp. When the heat inside the tube became too intense, the regulator short-circuited the platinum wire. As the tube cooled down and contracted, the electric circuit reconnected and the wire began to heat again and become luminous. This made the light get alternately bright and dim. That was not satisfactory.

Edison wanted a good vacuum inside his lamp

because the oxygen in air makes things burn more quickly.

One day Edison asked his helper, a man named Francis Jehl, "Have we got a pump around here?"

Jehl came up with a hand pump. Edison said to Ludwig Boehm, his glass blower: "Make me some completely enclosed bulbs shaped like a pear."

When these pear-shaped bulbs arrived on his work table, Edison put a spiral of platinum wire inside one and Jehl pumped the air out of the bulb. Edison turned on the current. The same electric current that before had produced five candle power (equal to the light of five candles), produced twenty-five candle power inside the vacuum—without melting the platinum.

This was the first milestone. Edison had established his theory. His work now was to obtain an even better vacuum and to find a cheap filament that would last. Platinum was too brittle and high-priced. He went to work on the pump first. He soon discovered that platinum at white heat made a gas that dimmed the light, so he had to find a way of dispelling the gas inside the vacuum of the bulb. He tried new ways of coiling the filament to give more resistance to the electric current and to decrease the size of its surface. This improved the lamp's lifespan.

Edison now began to test every known substance to find the best material for the filament. Week in and week out for more than a year, he and his workers patiently made filaments, inserted them in vacuum bulbs and turned on the current.

Edison's eyes began to suffer from constant exposure to light rays. To the intense pain was added the fear that, already deaf, he might also lose his eyesight. Also, his money was running out again. J. Pierpont Morgan and a group of bankers had organized the Edison Electric Light Company and advanced fifty thousand dollars to Edison for his experiments on the electric lamp. This money was about gone and he had received word there was to be no more.

One day Tom was pacing the second floor of his laboratory. One of his assistants, Charles Batchelor, was working in a corner of the shop. Edison ran his hands through his bushy hair, chewed on his unlighted cigar and stared at the lamp bulb hanging over his desk. Why couldn't he find the answer? He was almost discouraged but he remembered other times when he had been discouraged—such as the times he was trying to find the best substance for the telephone receiver and the phonograph. What had that been—lamp black! How about lamp black? Edison sat down and dug up some lamp black. He tried shaping it into a filament, but it wouldn't work. It was too brittle. He had thought about carbon at the beginning, but carbon united with air and burned out immediately, so he had discarded it.

"But that was before we had the vacuum bulb!" Edison thought.

"Hey, Batch," Edison called to his assistant. "Get me a spool of thread. I've got an idea."

Batchelor hunted up a spool of cotton thread. Edison folded the thread into the shape of a double hairpin. Then he carbonized the thread in the furnace. He proposed to put his carbon filament into the vacuum bulb.

For more than a month Edison and his assistants experimented with carbon filaments. Usually the filament broke up before they could get it out of the furnace. Other times it split in pieces while they were carrying it from the furnace to the table. And practically always it went to pieces while they were trying to insert it in the bulb. Finally, during the night of October 21, 1879, they managed to seal one of the delicate carbonized threads into the pear-shaped bulb and pump out the air.

Edison turned on the current. The lamp glowed like sunshine in the dusk of early autumn. They stared at it speechless, waiting for it to burn out. But it glowed on and on. They sat down to wait. Hours passed. Mealtimes came and went. All the other workers at Menlo Park heard about what was going on and began to file in on Sunday night to stare silently at the lamp. Suspense grew and the lamp burned on. Edison did not go home to sleep that night. He did not go home to sleep the next night. Nobody went home at all and as the light burned on, great rejoicing set in.

The first electric lamp burned for forty-five hours.

"If the lamp can burn for forty-five hours, I can make it burn for one hundred!" the inventor boasted.

Since lamps that burned fuel had been used to give light since prehistoric times, Edison always called his electric light bulb a lamp.

Edison had literally turned night into day. The electric light would affect everybody everywhere, and billions of people not yet born would benefit from it.

Edison continued his search for a better filament. He tried wood splinters, linen thread, paper, all kinds of grasses and human hair from a man's red beard. He finally decided that the most satisfactory filament was made of carbonized paper.

Edison did not tell the public about his successful lamp until just before Christmas. Then he invited Marshall Fox, a reporter on the *New York*

Replica of the first incandescent electric light. Edison made this model himself at the fiftieth-anniversary celebration in Dearborn, Michigan, in 1929.

Herald, to come and witness the experiment. Four days before Christmas the *Herald* printed the world-shaking story: "Edison's Light. The Great Inventor's Triumph. It Makes Light Without Gas or Flame." Most people, including Marshall Fox's boss, refused to believe it.

After the news of the electric lamp was published, people swarmed to Menlo Park. Edison then announced a demonstration of the incandescent lamp for New Year's Eve. This was one of the most unusual New Year's Eve parties ever given. The Pennsylvania Railroad transported more than three thousand persons to Menlo Park on the cold, snowy last night of the year 1879. They came from both New York and Philadelphia.

Edison had put some of his lamps along two wires strung between the leafless trees on the road leading from the railway station to his laboratory. As the trains began to pull in in the winter darkness, he pulled the switch and the electric lamps glowed like golden flowers, illuminating the road with a flood of light and casting long rays across the snow.

It is hard for us to imagine how exciting this was to people who had never seen an electric

Edison explaining his invention to visitors at Menlo Park on New Year's Eve, 1879. This drawing appeared in the New York *Daily Graphic*.

light. Many of them were sophisticated city people, dressed in their New Year's Eve party clothes; but they all gasped. It was the most beautiful sight they had ever seen. It was fairy-land!

Edison stood in the power house, watching the dynamo turn steam power into the electric current to light the lamps. He was wearing an old gray shirt, a flannel coat full of acid holes and some chalk-stained, dusty trousers. A broad-brimmed black felt hat sat on the back of his head. Some people took him for a coal stoker, so he had a good chance to listen to what they were saying.

"It's a miracle!"

"Did you ever see anything so beautiful?"

"He's a wizard! A wizard!"

Suddenly there was a scream and a commotion. A young lady was standing near the generators with her hair down her back.

"I'm sorry," Edison said. "The generators magnetized her hairpins and pulled them all out of her hair!" He apologized to the lady and gave her a silk kerchief to put on her head. "Maybe this will help," he said, but she fled back to the train.

The success of the New Year's Eve demonstration at Menlo Park created excitement all over the world. Cables, letters, telegrams and gifts descended on Edison. He was no longer just a hero, but the "American Wizard." Legends and myths and stories began to grow up around him. Thousands of superstitious people decided that the evening star was really an electric lamp that Edison had sent up in a balloon! Hundreds of people wrote to ask the inventor about the "Edison Star." Edison finally begged the *New York Herald* to publish his denial that he had anything to do with the stars. Many other wild stories were printed about Edison and his supernatural powers. Some of them are still told and retold.

Now Edison wanted to find a substance that would make a cheap, satisfactory and long-lasting filament for the electric bulb. And he wished to develop a way to produce and distribute electric power so cheaply and efficiently that everybody in the world could use it.

He was determined to make a bulb that would cost less than fifty cents. He went on trying out many kinds of vegetable fibers—new kinds of wood and new kinds of cloth, grass stems, bark of trees—searching for the best possible filament.

One day Edison noticed a palm-leaf fan in the laboratory. Palm-leaf fans were common household objects in those days. He picked it up and looked at it. The edge was bound with a long, thin strip of bamboo. He stripped off a tough, outer segment and carbonized it in the oven. It worked better than anything he had tried. He was wildly elated. He began to study everything ever printed about bamboo and to organize expeditions to locate all kinds of special varieties.

Edison sent a man named William Moore to travel the length and breadth of Japan and China. Moore furnished the bamboo used in Edison lamps for several years. Edison later sent a man named Frank McGowan to search the vicinity of the Amazon. McGowan pressed his search across South America, not removing his clothes for ninety-eight days, and engaging in battles with many wild beasts. Edison sent a man named James Ricalton to Ceylon and Burma, across the Himalayas and through India. In all, Edison's bamboo expeditions cost over $100,000.

When Ricalton, his last explorer, returned with two excellent bamboo samples, after a year of hazardous travel which had taken him all the way around the world, Edison was waiting on the pier when his boat docked.

"Hello," Edison greeted him, shaking hands. "Did you find it?"

Almost before Ricalton could say yes, Edison hurried on about his business. Ricalton was soon told that Edison was already using a filament

A page of Edison's patent for the electric lamp

T. A. EDISON.
Electric-Lamp.

No. 223,898.   Patented Jan. 27, 1880.

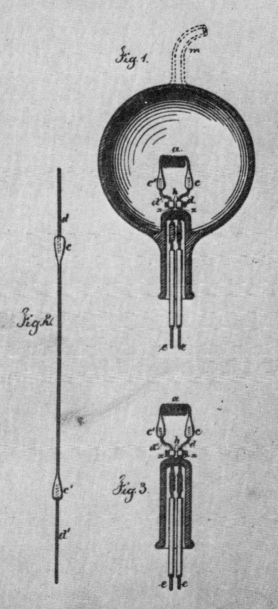

Fig. 1.

Fig. 2.

Fig. 3.

Inventor
Thomas A. Edison

Witnesses
Chas. H. Smith

made by carbonizing a fine thread of cellulose squirted out of a die—the way nylon is made today. So Ricalton's long year's work had been unnecessary.

Edison continued to receive tributes from all over the world for the electric lamp. In 1881 it was displayed at the Paris Electrical Exposition, where Edison was awarded five gold medals. His electric lamp also attracted great attention the following year at the Crystal Palace Electrical Exposition in London, where it was displayed in a magnificent chandelier composed of 213 electric lights.

In October 1880, Edison had set up the first factory for the manufacture of electric lights. It was located in a building across the road from the laboratory in Menlo Park. The manufacturing business was started with an investment of only ten thousand dollars. Edison's associates, Batchelor, Johnson and Upton, invested small sums in the business and became junior partners. Within a year, the company was employing 133 men and turning out 1,000 lamps a day. To launch this business, Edison was forced to sell off much of his personal property and stocks and to risk all he had earned in years of hard work. During the winter he traveled back and forth between New York and Menlo Park, making financial arrangements and keeping the factory going at the same time.

One cold day in February, he decided that he had better stay in New York. As he looked around the scattered shops and buildings of Menlo Park, he said, "My work here is done." He felt a twinge of melancholy.

The Wizard of Menlo Park was now thirty-four years old.

7

Father of Motion Pictures

Tom Edison knew that an incandescent lamp would do the world little good unless he found a way to install systems of electric power to provide current. He could manufacture thousands of bulbs, but without cheap electric power they were of little use. Edison moved to New York City to build a system to generate and distribute electric power on a large scale.

Edison had always been something of a showman. The first thing he did in New York was to rent a mansion at 65 Fifth Avenue, just below

14th Street, for his place of business. At that time, most of the city's fine houses were to be found in this neighborhood. Edison's headquarters had beautiful rugs and carpets and fine furniture and was unlike any place the Wizard had ever worked before. Edison set up a generator in the basement to run a lighting system for the house, and he installed a large supply of his electric lights in a number of crystal chandeliers. He burned these late into the night. People drove their horses and carriages by the house just to marvel at the "electroliers."

The mansion at 65 Fifth Avenue was the birthplace of the Edison Electric Illuminating Company of New York (now known as the Consolidated Edison Company). If you can imagine a city without power plants and without wires and without most of the electric equipment that we take for granted, you can understand what Edison's life was like in the years after he invented the lamp. Meters, fuses, sockets, switches, tubes, conductors, junction boxes and dozens of other things had to be invented and made before the system could work. Most of Edison's men from the Menlo Park shops were put in charge of new companies to make these items.

Edison bought an ironworks on Goerck Street in New York and started the Edison Machine Works, where he made dynamos. Sigmund Bergmann, who had worked for Edison in Newark, set up a shop to produce small equipment. John Kruesi took over the Electric Tube Company on Washington Street. At 257 Pearl Street, Edison started the first power plant to generate and distribute electric power on a large scale.

Everything about the system had to be thought through and put together by Edison and his men. Nowhere could they buy what they needed. Nobody else could make what they had to have. Edison took out 360 patents on inventions which were concerned with the generation and distribution of electricity for light and power. He soon had more than 2,000 people working for him.

Meanwhile, Edison had to keep the public interested in his lamp until he could prove its usefulness. He had to break down the kind of dislike that many people have for anything new. He was willing to try the lamp anywhere it would get attention. Once he organized a parade in which the marchers wore helmets with an electric light attached to the front, operated by a tiny portable steam engine and dynamo inside the helmet. He planned a spectacle in Niblo's Gardens, a famous theater, where the girls in the ballet wore electric lights on their foreheads and carried wands with electric lights at the tips. Each lamp was connected by almost invisible wires to a dynamo and steam engine Edison had built in the basement of the theater. Four hundred electric lamps were used in this spectacle, which was the talk of the town.

The first American theater lighted by electric lights was located in Boston. Tom and Mary Edison attended the grand opening in December 1882. The Governor of Massachusetts and the Mayor of Boston were also present. In the middle of the performance of *Iolanthe* by Gilbert and Sullivan, Edison noticed that the electric lights were growing dimmer. He dashed out of his box and rushed to the basement, where he found the fireman of the steam engine asleep. Edison tore off his tailcoat and began to shovel coal into the engine to build up the steam. As soon as he had raised the power enough to bring the lights up, he dusted off his hands, put on his coat and ran back to the box before the curtain went down.

But far more important was Edison's plan to lay his system of wires to bring electric light to New York City. He was determined to lay his wires in underground pipes to avoid the dangers of short circuits and shocks. Many people felt that such a system was certain to blow up the city. Edison had to persuade the city officials of the safety of his plan by giving them another demonstration at Menlo Park, followed by a fancy dinner. And as usual, he needed money. He had to win the bankers to his side by promising to make electric

In the spring of 1882, *Harper's Weekly* pictured Edison (far left) working on the installation of tubing for electric wires beneath New York City streets.

lights cheaper than gas lights. Then he had to actually lay the system.

The part of New York that Edison planned to light first ran from Canal Street to a point just south of Wall Street and from Broadway to the East River. The plan called for fourteen miles of underground mains and the wiring of all houses and other buildings where the electric light had been accepted.

Edison took personal charge of the job. He was everywhere at once. He could be found down in the mud and muck of the ditches, helping to install the pipes with his own hands, an old stovepipe hat on the back of his head. He had never thought much about sleeping at night, and now he forgot it altogether. He hardly ever saw Mary Edison and the children. He snatched catnaps in the middle of the night in the cellar of the Pearl Street Station, curled up on a pile of iron pipes.

Edison drove his crews as he drove himself. He never asked them to do anything he wouldn't or couldn't do, and as a result they loved him. They laid one thousand feet of mains a day in the hard, frozen earth of New York City.

In Edison's spare time, he designed and built the largest dynamo generator ever known to man. He had simplified the operation and increased the speed of the generator. He filed several new patents on this monster machine.

On Monday, September 4, 1882, Edison was ready to demonstrate his new system. It was a year and a half since he had moved to New York City to undertake the great project. The mains were in the ground, the connections were all made, the big dynamo was installed and it only remained to pull the master switch.

Edison's companies were all deeply in debt. His men were exhausted. His family had almost forgotten what he looked like. If the system didn't work, he could imagine what would happen. The light might fail! He spent a sleepless Sunday night, checking every detail. On Monday afternoon he went home and got dressed in a new frock coat, striped trousers and top hat, which he had bought to impress his bankers.

"I was a little nervous," Edison admitted later.

The switch was pulled at a signal from Edison. All over New York hundreds of electric lights bloomed like flowers. For the first time in history a city glowed with steady light, snuffing out the darkness. The system was a success.

Edison might have been expected to take the night off to celebrate his triumph. When the newspaper reporters started looking for him, they couldn't find him. Somebody said he was last seen going toward Pearl Street. When the press got to the power plant, he was there with his coat off and his collar off and his striped trousers grimy with grease.

"This engine was making too much racket," he said. "I thought I'd better fix it."

In later years thousands of electric power plants were built all over the United States. Hundreds of new companies were organized and Edison eventually became a millionaire. But he scarcely noticed it. He had gotten interested in other things—including electric transportation.

At that time all the streetcars in cities were pulled by horses. Horse cars were slow, expensive and hard on the horse. Horses could work only about three or four hours a day. In hot weather they fell in their tracks. These drawbacks, as well as the increased speed of electric cars, brought about public interest in electric transportation.

Edison had built an electric railroad at Menlo Park to amuse himself. He had laid two rails 3½ feet apart on the ground, without any grading to even them. He installed a dynamo on a flat car and then added two open cars with awnings and seats for passengers. The track was a half-mile long. The train often jumped the track and threw everybody off into the dirt, but this was part of the fun. The electric train achieved a speed of forty miles an hour.

Edison continued to tinker with it. Near Menlo Park he built a three-mile track with switches and sidings and grades. He later installed a third rail, which supplied the train with electric current from a dynamo at a distance, and he invented an electric brake. As usual, people said the invention was dangerous and that the third rail would be short-circuited by bad weather. They said that no dynamo would ever be able to run a real railroad engine. Edison turned his deaf ears to this talk.

But it took a collision between steam engines in the tunnel leading into the Grand Central Depot in New York to establish the electric railroad. The New York Central adopted Edison's

The electric railway at Menlo Park, with Charles Batchelor as engineer

ideas and began to use electric engines on their underground tracks. This brought relief to everybody who had had to ride through tunnels of smoke made by steam engines underground. Other great railroad companies followed the lead and adopted the electric engine. Edison's experiments with electric trains were the last he ever made at Menlo Park.

Edison's New York home was a house facing Gramercy Park, where Marion, Tom, Jr., and Will went to play behind the big iron fence. Mary Edison enjoyed the life of the city and gave tea parties and dinners, which she could rarely persuade her husband to attend. Marion went to a private school—against her father's will. Because of his own unusual schooling, Edison did not believe in formal schools. He tried to get his daughter to stay home and read the books he had read as a child. But Marion was a young girl, not a future inventor, and she found these books very hard to read. Edison wanted his sons to learn to work with their hands.

The Edison family spent their summers at Menlo Park in their old home. In the summer of 1884, Mary Edison became ill with typhoid fever. Although her sister, Alice, nursed her faithfully, she did not get better, and Edison rushed to her side from New York. In the early morning hours of August 9, 1884, Mary Edison died at the age of twenty-nine. Her husband stumbled out of the room in tears, almost unable to tell his children the terrible news.

After that, Edison could hardly bear to look at Menlo Park. He seemed to hate the place that had been the scene of so many of his triumphs. The laboratory fell into ruin and was finally used as a stable for cows.

Mary Edison had asked little of Tom and she had worshiped him. He had not had much time for home life, but Mary had always been there. Now Edison became terribly lonely. Perhaps he felt remorse. He did not know his children very well and he did not really know how to get on with young children. The children stayed with their grandmother Stilwell in New York or with their Aunt Alice in Menlo Park. Soon the two boys—Thomas Alva, Jr., who was eight, and William, who was six—went to live with their Aunt Alice. Edison did not visit them often.

But his thirteen-year-old daughter, Marion, became his constant companion. She would go down to the machine works and sit and talk with him to try to cheer him up. He took her to the Metropolitan Opera and hired a horse and carriage to take her driving in Central Park. She planned meals he liked, bought his cigars and learned to play all his favorite songs on the piano. She did her best to fill her mother's place.

Edison's loneliness soon drove him to do what

he had never done before—to go out in society. Everybody wanted the famous Thomas Edison to come to parties, but he had never paid any attention to such invitations before. He had always liked to wear old clothes and sloppy shoes and work around a machine shop. Now he bought a new evening suit with a starched shirt and shoes that pinched his feet. And he stopped chewing tobacco, since he could find no place to spit in a parlor. He went to musical comedies, and plays, and to house parties and yachting parties, where people just played. Sometimes he got very tired of playing and would go to his room and read the *Encyclopaedia Britannica* to relax.

It was at a house party in Boston that he met a beautiful girl named Mina Miller. She was the daughter of Lewis Miller, a manufacturer of agricultural implements who lived in Akron, Ohio. Mina was only eighteen years old, but she understood inventors. When she was introduced to the 38-year-old Edison, she did not flatter him with compliments or make a fuss over him, as people usually did. She simply sat down at the piano and played and sang. Edison could not get his eyes or his mind off Mina Miller. He knew that he was in love.

Mina Miller Edison, the inventor's second wife, at about the time of their marriage

Edison wooed Mina by telephone and telegraph. When she spent the summer in Chautauqua, New York, he went to Chautauqua. For some time he did not invent anything except love letters.

Mina was only a few years older than Edison's daughter, Marion, and she had another suitor. But Edison, as usual, won out. On February 24, 1886, they were married in the Miller home in Akron at a beautiful wedding, attended by Edison's old friends and co-workers.

For his new bride, Thomas Edison bought an estate named Glenmont in West Orange, in Essex County, New Jersey. The red brick mansion, with chimneys and gables and balconies, was set in the middle of thirteen acres of land, landscaped like a park. The stately house was furnished in the height of luxury with fine furniture and Oriental rugs. It had a large drawing room, a library, an enormous dining room, a great hall and many bedrooms. On the second floor Edison had a den, where he could work. Marion, Tom and William Edison soon came to live at Glenmont with their father and stepmother.

Meanwhile, Edison had begun the construction of a laboratory in West Orange, near his new home. Now that he was able to buy whatever he wanted, he determined to make the Orange laboratory the finest private laboratory the world had ever known. The new laboratory complex consisted of six brick buildings with a library housing ten thousand books, carpenter shops, glass-blowing rooms, machine shops, dynamo and motor rooms, drafting rooms, and a stock-room which Edison had always dreamed of owning. It had drawers from floor to ceiling and contained every possible kind of material that an inventor could imagine wanting—everything from macaroni and hog bristles and the skins of snakes to platinum and precious stones. Edison offered a reward of one dollar to any employee who could think of an item the stockroom didn't have. He was rather upset to have an office boy ask for a clothespin one day—and to discover there was no clothespin in the stockroom. Edison paid the reward.

Edison now entered another time of great personal satisfaction. His family was back under one roof, and there was a new baby, Madeleine. Tom and Mina Edison had much in common. They both loved to read and they both enjoyed music. Edison gave up tight shoes and stopped going to parties. He refused to wear stiff shirts, and put on his old linen duster again. Mina Edison was young and she must have missed social life, but she did not insist on Tom's being a social lion except when she felt it was absolutely

The Edison exhibit at the Paris International Exposition in 1889

necessary. She felt it was necessary in 1889, when the French government invited Edison to attend the Paris International Exposition.

Edison growled but he accepted the invitation

and took his 22-year-old wife to Paris. His daughter Marion joined them. Edison and his attractive family took Paris by storm. Never since the time of Benjamin Franklin, another inventor, had there been so much excitement about an American in Paris. When Edison attended the Paris Opera in President Carnot's box, the house was draped with American flags. As he and his wife and daughter came in, "The Star-Spangled Banner" was played and the hall rang with "Vive Edison!"

The city of Paris presented him with a gold medal. The French Society of Engineers gave him a great banquet in the newly completed Eiffel Tower. At this dinner the great French composer Charles François Gounod played a composition written in honor of Edison's visit. President Carnot decorated Edison with the Legion of Honor.

The Edisons traveled all over Europe and were received with the same sort of excitement in Berlin, London and Rome, where King Umberto conferred upon the inventor the insignia of a Grand Officer of the Crown of Italy. This honor made Edison a count, but he was always embarrassed when he was addressed by his title. He remained as modest as ever and said that the praise and glory given him in Europe belonged not to him but to America. Edison enjoyed his European travels but said he ate so many big dinners he would never be the same. However, he remained the same. He weighed 182 pounds for many years and he never had to have his clothes fitted by a tailor. They were made on a form exactly his size and his size didn't change.

Edison enjoyed himself in Europe that summer of 1889, for he had just sold a large portion of his interests in his various companies to a group of bankers headed by Henry Villard, representing European interests, and the Morgan bank of New York. This resulted in the founding of the Edison General Electric Company (now known as General Electric), of which Villard was elected president. Edison kept a small amount of stock and was one of the directors of the company. But he had little authority in the management of the great company built on his inventions.

Edison was at last relieved of financial strain, but he could not bear to be idle. He began a new project. He was determined to invent a new iron-ore milling process which would make it possible to use low-grade ore. Edison spent ten years on this venture. As usual, he stayed in the field and worked with the men, but nothing he could do seemed to make his process economical. At times Edison lost thousands of dollars a day, and he spent most of the fortune he had accumulated. When he dismantled the works, he owed money.

We now know that Edison was seventy years

ahead of his time. Today, with the exhaustion of high-grade ore, his method is coming into use.

Edison was no more depressed by defeat than he had been made arrogant by success. He said he had never had a better time—and turned his attention to something new.

One day when he was riding a train from Orange to New York, he noticed that the landscape, rushing by the window as the train speeded on, had the effect of moving in the opposite direction. He had always been fascinated by movement and he began to wonder if a moving-picture machine could be figured out. He said he wished to invent a machine that would do for the eye what the phonograph had done for the ear.

Now Edison wanted to learn everything about photography. He studied the life and work of Daguerre, who had invented photography in France more than a half-century before. He recalled the zoetrope, a mechanical toy containing a wheel fitted with dozens of small pictures enclosed in a box with slots. When the wheel was revolved before the slots, the observer received an impression of continuous action.

Edison decided to try to make a camera that would record both motion and sound. He was fortunate to have as a laboratory assistant at this time a young Englishman named William K. L.

Dickson, who was interested in amateur photography and was always experimenting with it in the laboratory. He and Dickson put their heads together. Then Dickson went off to gather up every possible kind of photographic material for the laboratory storeroom.

Experiments on the moving-picture camera were started in Room 5 of the West Orange laboratory behind locked doors. Dickson made a series of tiny photographs, as small as 1/32 of an inch, of persons and objects in motion, on the dry plates then in use in photography. Edison became convinced that the glass used for photographic plates was too brittle and stiff for the purpose of moving pictures. He wanted a flexible material. He began to experiment with celluloid, coated with a photographic emulsion, which he bought from John Carbutt, a photography pioneer in New York. Edison wrapped the celluloid sheet around a cylinder.

But he found that he could not devise a viewing mechanism to focus satisfactorily on the curved surface of the cylinder. So he and Dickson decided to cut the celluloid into narrow pieces and glue them together to make one continuous strip, which could be moved—frame by frame— across the front of the camera.

George Eastman was already experimenting in Rochester with film for his rapid-action Kodak, and Edison sent Dickson to Rochester to get a sample of the film. At Edison's request, Eastman later made a fifty-foot length of celluloid film, instead of the usual short pieces required for a Kodak.

"Now we've got it!" Edison said when he saw the long film. "Let's get to work."

Edison designed a machine for feeding the film into the camera at a given rate of speed. He obtained a patent on the first moving-picture machine, called the Kinetograph, in 1891. He also developed a projector called the Vitascope (invented by Thomas Armat), which enlarged the small pictures by sending light from an arc lamp through a magnifying lens onto a screen. Originally Edison had planned to use the same machine for photographing and projecting, but this proved impractical.

The Wizard's original idea was that pictures should not only move but talk. He planned to combine the Kinetograph and the phonograph. He had dreams of photographing and recording a full-length opera at the Metropolitan Opera House. If he could have accomplished this, silent pictures might never have existed. But the difficulties proved too great even for Edison.

As soon as the practicality of the moving-picture camera was established, a new building went up at the West Orange laboratory. It looked like a barn with a sloping roof, but the whole building could be revolved on a track, so that the

stage and the camera could make use of every bit of sunlight and daylight. The building was painted black on the inside and was walled with black roofing paper on the outside. It became known as the Black Maria. It was the first moving-picture studio in the world.

Edison really enjoyed this invention. He had always loved the opera, theater and vaudeville, and now the great actors and dancers and entertainers came to West Orange to be in moving pictures. Gentleman Jim Corbett boxed a few rounds for the camera. Circus acts were photographed. Loie Fuller, a famous dancer, performed. Edison staged fencing exhibitions and a sham battle. He produced his films for commercial use in his Kinetoscope machine, which was operated by feeding coins into the machine and looking through a little window at the moving picture.

Edison's children, including his third son, Charles, who had been born on August 3, 1890, loved the Black Maria. (Edison's sixth and last child, Theodore, was born in 1898.) No treat was greater than a trip to the moving-picture factory.

Charles was especially fond of going to work with his father, and often accompanied him to the laboratory. Edison never shortened his working

Edison with an early movie projector

143

hours to accommodate Charles. Edison had found a cozy new place to sleep himself. He would curl up on the flat surface of his big roll-top desk and pull the top down over him.

When Charles got sleepy, Edison advised him to sleep on the floor but to always get under a

A scene from *The Great Train Robbery*, one of Edison's most popular movies

table so he wouldn't be stepped on. When Mina Edison heard this, she was furious.

"Why, it's not clean," she said. "You spit your tobacco there!"

Edison couldn't understand why she was so upset.

Edison predicted that, in twenty years, children would be taught by motion pictures instead of books. He wasn't entirely right, but he recognized immediately the great power and future of moving pictures.

Once more the American Wizard had made an invention that would affect the whole world forever.

8

Dauntless Wizard

Edison achieved great success through native genius, hard work and his patient method of trial and error. He also experienced numerous failures. He could be wrong and he was often stubborn about his wrong ideas. He made mistakes of all sorts.

One of his failings was impatience with financial matters. Although making money was not Edison's ultimate goal, he had to have money to live on, to support his family and to put his ideas into operation. But Edison was irritated by business. He preferred to turn it over to others.

He built a $100,000 movie studio in the Bronx and became one of the leading manufacturers of motion pictures. On one occasion he made an agreement with his competitors—an agreement that eventually resulted in millions of dollars in royalties and other revenues. When this agreement was signed, Edison refused to take part in the discussion. He curled up on a cot in the corner of his library in West Orange and took a nap. When he was awakened, he signed the agreement without reading it and went back to the laboratory.

He did not believe in the flat disk record for the phonograph, because the cylinder record provided better sound reproduction. Long after the flat disk became more popular—because it could be stored easily—he kept on making the cylinder record.

Some of Edison's discoveries in pure science were important contributions to wireless telegraphy, radio, and the later science of electronics, including television. His carbon telephone transmitter proved to be the basis for the microphone used in radio broadcasting.

Although Edison believed in wireless telegraphy, he had less faith in the future of radio. He thought that people would want to choose their own music to play on their own phonographs.

Edison sold two of his wireless-telegraphy patents to the Marconi Wireless Telegraphy Company. Guglielmo Marconi once came to visit Edison, as many scientists did, to worship at his shrine. Edison happened to be alone at home. He took Marconi to the kitchen and made him a cheese sandwich. They talked all day—but Edison never got around to liking radio.

Another modern development that Edison never fully accepted was the automobile as we know it—with an internal-combustion engine powered by gasoline. In 1900, when the automobile age was beginning, Tom Edison had reason to think that the "electric" would take the place of the horse. Electric cars were in the majority, and they were being made by former carriage- and wagon-makers. Electric cars were light, quiet and clean, compared to the noisy, heavy, smelly gas-engine cars. On the other hand, the "electrics" were powered with lead-acid storage batteries, which had to be recharged constantly, so that drivers of electrics could not get very far from a power plant. The radius of these cars was limited to a few miles. The batteries were expensive, hard to charge and they corroded rapidly.

Edison decided to build a better storage battery. He had a vision of a storage battery small enough to be carried in a suitcase, light enough to

148

hold in one hand, cheap enough for everybody to own and so strong that it would last forever. All he had to do was invent it!

He began with his usual excitement. He wanted to find a combination of chemicals that would work better than lead with acid. In his first experiments he worked with copper oxide, iron oxide and an alkaline solution. When this combination did not work out, he tried hundreds of other chemicals. Eighteen months went by. Edison had done thousands of experiments with the storage battery and he was no further along than he had been the first day.

Finally, in 1903 Edison decided to use nickel hydrate with graphite for the positive element and a form of iron for the negative element in his alkaline battery. He set up an electrical machine in the laboratory to jolt the batteries to see if they would work while moving over rough roads. He even made a habit of throwing the batteries out of the second-story window of the laboratory, just to be sure they could take abuse and stand up. He tried them out in buggies on the roughest roads in New Jersey. He believed he had solved the problem.

In 1904 he built a factory to produce the batteries at Silver Lake, New Jersey, and started a publicity campaign. Edison claimed that his battery was light, foolproof, could be charged forever. He said they would stand any kind of

punishment. He said that his storage battery would bring down the price of automobiles, so that everybody could own one, and that the storage battery could be used for any number of other things, such as lighting a house. He had an electric motor installed in a red buggy, with one of his storage batteries supplying the current. He claimed the electric was so simple to operate that his twelve-year-old son could drive it.

People rushed to buy electric cars with the Wizard's storage battery. Then the trouble started. The batteries leaked while the cars were running. The power dropped constantly, so the cars couldn't be trusted to move on. And they would then bog down in mud.

The nickel-iron storage battery was a failure. Edison shut down his factory and took back all the defective batteries, repaying purchasers out of his own pocket.

"They may not be perfect," one of his assistants remonstrated, "but they are the best batteries you can buy. Why should we quit making them?"

"They are not satisfactory to *me*," Edison said. He went back to work on the storage battery.

He threw his entire laboratory force into this investigation. The years went by and the number

Edison and his son Theodore at Glenmont, riding in an automobile powered by an Edison storage battery of experiments made was record-breaking. They ran well over 10,000. They were also heart-breaking. The storage battery did not yield up its secret. It could not be made entirely foolproof.

Edison went on striving and trying to keep up the morale of his men. But he himself was discouraged. In the winter of 1905 he developed mastoiditis. A dangerous operation was performed to save his life, but afterward he was almost stone deaf.

For many years, he had gone to Florida for an annual winter vacation, but that year he refused to go. He went back to his laboratory.

After one of the thousands of tests had turned out badly, one of his men came to him and said: "It won't work. The whole thing is a waste of time and money!"

"Is that all you have to say for yourself?" Edison demanded.

"It's a problem without a solution," another associate said.

"If the Lord made a problem, he also made a solution," Edison said. "Don't tell me the Lord made something impossible."

In 1907 Edison was sixty. His thick, unruly hair had turned white. He had always been pale, but now his face was ghostly. The panic of 1907 had made money scarce. Rolls-Royce had produced a gasoline-driven automobile that had stood up for ten thousand miles.

Edison and some of his assistants, known as the Insomnia Squad, in the West Orange laboratory

Edison still believed in the electric car. He plodded on with his storage battery.

In 1908 Edison's battery was finally ready. It had taken ten years of his life and $1,000,000 of his money. But it was now too late for the electric automobile, which reacted badly to cold weather, snow drifts and muddy roads. A few companies made electric runabouts and light trucks which were used for a few years, but the gasoline-driven motor, more powerful and cheaper to operate, forged ahead.

The battery, however, had many other uses. For many years it was the principal money-maker of Thomas A. Edison, Inc. Still manufactured today essentially as it was in 1908, it is used on railroad trains, steamships and lift trucks, for miners' safety caps and mountaintop airplane beacons, as well as for electric power on isolated farms.

Although electric automobiles did not replace the horse, the age of electricity had arrived with the twentieth century. When Edison's inventions were first beginning to come into general use, Theodore Roosevelt was President. The St. Louis World's Fair of 1904 displayed Edison's miracles to the public. In October 1905, the Wright Brothers flew an airplane 24 miles in 38 minutes. In 1906 there were several natural catastrophes—an earthquake in Formosa, the eruption of Mount Vesuvius, the Italian volcano, and the San Francisco earthquake and fire. Wealthy Americans were entertaining with costume balls and elaborate parties, purchasing art masterpieces, buying cars and yachts, building palaces, hiring servants, traveling to Europe so that their daughters could meet counts and dukes, whom they often married. They went to the opera house to hear Caruso sing and to the vaudeville theater to see Lillian Russell. Workingmen began to complain about wages and hours and to ask for laws to protect themselves. Women began to campaign for a chance to vote with men.

And in 1904 Edison's electric lamp was a quarter of a century old.

On February 11, 1904, the American Institute of Electrical Engineers gave the Wizard a birthday party with five hundred guests at the Waldorf-Astoria Hotel to celebrate the silver anniversary of the electric light. Edison was called America's greatest and most useful citizen. Electric lights were used everywhere at this party. Even the ice cream was frozen in the shape of a light bulb!

After World War I broke out in Europe in 1914, Edison was invited by the Secretary of the Navy to become a member of the Navy Consulting Board, a group of America's famous scientists who were asked to advise the government about preparedness for war. Edison became president of the board. He was so deaf that everything said at the meetings had to be tapped out on his knee in Morse code.

After America entered World War I, Edison spent most of his time working on machines to detect submarines and inventions for submarine warfare. Edison submitted forty-five inventions to the navy during World War I. "Perfectly good ones," Edison later said, "but they were all pigeon-holed!" All these things frustrated the inventor, who had never taken no for an answer. He had a habit of making things work—by trying and trying again.

Edison was not daunted by failure. When he had tried everything to make one of his ideas work, or when he could not persuade other people to accept his conclusions, or when he realized he was wrong, he did not feel sorry for himself, sulk or grow bitter. He went to work on another idea.

Thomas Edison's optimism was one of the inspiring things about him. In 1914 his concrete factory buildings at West Orange were completely gutted by a disastrous fire. Edison was chiefly interested in the fact that the buildings he had constructed of poured concrete remained standing. He had been experimenting with poured-concrete houses, and this fire proved that the material had one great advantage. "It just shows that we are making the best cement in the world," he said.

The library at the West Orange laboratory. Behind Edison's roll-top desk is a model of a poured-concrete house, his pioneering idea for prefabricated housing. The statue behind Edison is called "The Triumph of Light."

The loss to Edison represented by this fire could hardly be measured. The buildings were not insured, and money alone could not have paid for the machinery they contained. Much of it was unique and had been built for his purposes. But Edison knew from childhood experience that fire was always a hazard. "Into each life some rain must fall," he said, quoting Henry Wadsworth Longfellow, one of his favorite poets. He then sat up all night drawing plans for a new factory.

The next morning he hired fifteen hundred men to clear away the debris and took personal charge of the operation, although he was already an old man. Foundations of new buildings began to rise while the ruins of the old were still smoking. In less than a month the first building of the new laboratory was operating.

It is believed that Henry Ford came to his rescue with a loan. In earlier years, Henry Ford had worked as chief engineer in the Detroit Edison Company's power house. A thin, gangling youth, Ford was experimenting at home with a gas buggy. Edison was his idol. Ford's greatest dream was to meet the Wizard in person and talk about his invention. At last he met his hero at a convention of Edison companies.

Henry Ford was shy and Edison was deaf. The Wizard cupped his ear to listen to Ford talk about his car, and when he had finished he advised Ford: "Keep at it!" Ford was excited and felt that

Edison's approval almost guaranteed the success of his invention. He went back to Detroit and kept at it. He said his meeting with Edison was the turning point in his career. But Edison is reported to have said that he didn't think Ford was quite bright when he first met him.

Ford proved him wrong. He invented a fifteen-horsepower, four-cylinder car which required only one gallon of gasoline to run twenty miles. The car cost six hundred dollars and the public rushed to buy it. But Ford never ceased to look up to Edison and to cultivate his acquaintance.

When Edison had an opportunity to know Ford better, their friendship ripened. Henry Ford and his wife came to Fort Myers, Florida, to see Tom and Mina Edison, and the Edisons visited the Fords in Detroit. John Burroughs, the great American naturalist, joined them one winter in Florida, and the three men toured the Everglades. Through Ford, Edison met Harvey Firestone, a rubber manufacturer who made tires for Ford's automobiles, and they struck up a friendship. The four men planned a long camping trip by automobile through New York State and New England. When the time came, Ford was unable to get away; but Burroughs, Firestone and Edison took the trip.

Edison made all the arrangements. They traveled in a six-cylinder automobile with a Model T truck behind carrying supplies. They went to

Lake George, New York, and over the Adirondack Mountains into Vermont. They slept in the open, cooked over a campfire and washed in the nearest creek. At night they sat around the campfire talking about life and telling stories.

The four friends went on many of these camping trips through the years. Edison loved such gypsy outings. He always sat in the front seat of the car with the driver. The mountain roads in those days were rough and dangerous, but Edison was never so happy as when the car could be got up to a speed of forty miles an hour.

The friends enjoyed the trips very much until reporters began to follow them and people gathered and stared at them. Edison always slept in his clothes and roughed it. In spite of all he had said about not needing sleep, sometimes he didn't get up on his camping trips until ten o'clock in the morning.

It was on one of these camping trips that Ford and Firestone expressed worries about a shortage of rubber and the increased prices of rubber imported from the tropics. They suggested that Tom Edison ought to do something about developing an alternate source for rubber. With the

Harvey Firestone examining one of Edison's experimental rubber-bearing plants at his botanical gardens in Fort Myers, Florida

need for rubber tires on automobiles, the demand for rubber had increased steadily.

Edison liked the idea. He was never so happy as when he was working on a new invention. In 1927 he began his last great experiments. He started the way he always had—by reading everything he could find on the subject of rubber, beginning with its discovery in the jungles of South America four centuries before. At Seminole Lodge, his house in Florida, he started a great rubber library. He then began to send out expeditions to bring in plants that might yield rubber. He tried everything from a honeysuckle vine to cactus. Edison investigated more than seventeen thousand weeds, vines, shrubs and trees, finding some rubber in about twelve hundred different plants. Forty of these plants had fairly large quantities of rubber. He finally decided that the goldenrod was the most likely plant for cultivation in the United States.

Edison, by crossbreeding, developed a goldenrod plant fourteen feet tall which yielded 12 percent latex. He believed that with the proper cultivation of this plant he would be able to harvest a hundred pounds of rubber from an acre of goldenrod. However, Edison's rubber was expensive to make and not as good as the rubber imported from the tropics. The old inventor hid his disappointment but he did not give up.

"Give me five years," he said, "and the United States will raise her own rubber."

But Edison was doomed to failure with his rubber experiments. He didn't have five years to continue the search.

On October 21, 1929, the whole world celebrated the fiftieth birthday of the electric light. Henry Ford had prepared a shrine to Edison's labors at Greenfield Village in Dearborn, Michigan, where he had restored the original Menlo Park laboratory on soil brought from New Jersey by railroad flatcars. This shrine was dedicated as part of the fiftieth-anniversary celebration. Tom and Mina Edison traveled to Dearborn with the President of the United States, Herbert Hoover, and Mrs. Hoover, to take part in the ceremonies.

During the long day, honors were heaped on the great inventor. He and Francis Jehl re-enacted the birth of the electric light. He was praised and flattered.

"Well, Mr. Edison, how do you like your laboratory?" Henry Ford asked his friend.

"I'll tell you, Henry, it's not quite right," Edison said.

"What's wrong with it?" Ford asked, disappointed.

"The floor's too clean!" Edison said.

At a great dinner that evening in Edison's

164

honor, President Hoover praised him as America's greatest national possession. Edison stood up in the storm of applause to respond. He was deeply moved. The tears sprang to his eyes and he swayed. He made a short speech, expressing his thanks, and sat down. Mina noticed that he slumped in his chair and his face was gray. President Hoover's physician was called and persuaded Edison to leave the table. A shot of Adrenalin restored him and he was able to finish the evening.

But he knew that something was wrong. He went to a doctor, who discovered that he had gastric ulcers, diabetes and uremic poisoning. Edison flouted the idea that anything could be really wrong with him. He had rarely been sick in his life. He said he was in good shape for a man eighty-two years old. He went back to Fort Myers and started working on the goldenrod rubber plant again.

He never stopped working. He improved the machinery for extracting the latex from the goldenrod, and he produced enough rubber so Firestone could make four vulcanized tires for Edison's automobile. But time was running out.

Henry Ford (center) and Francis Jehl (right) watching Edison re-enact the birth of the electric light at the fiftieth-anniversary celebration

On August 1, 1931, he collapsed. He was well past eighty-four and nobody expected him to live much longer. But Edison got back on his feet and struggled to resume his work.

Now his strength ebbed away. As he had fought throughout the long battle of his life, he fought gallantly on. The light still burned. But on October 15 he sank into a coma and in the early morning hours of Sunday, October 18, the spark was snuffed out. The dauntless Edison was dead.

On the fifty-second anniversary of the electric light, October 21, 1931, Edison was buried under an oak tree in Rosedale Cemetery, near Glenmont. It was suggested that President Hoover order all electric current in the United States to be turned off for one minute in tribute to the inventor. But the greatest tribute that could be paid Edison occurred when it was decided that this would be impossible. So great was his contribution to our civilization that it would be dangerous to try to get along without it—even for one minute.

9

Down-to-Earth
Dreamer

Thomas Edison was often called the greatest
genius of his age. There are few men of any age
who have had a more direct effect on the lives of
everyone everywhere than the inventor of the
first practical electric light. But Edison never
considered it a compliment to be described as a
genius.

"There is no such thing as genius," Edison
said. "What people choose to call genius is simply
hard work—one per cent inspiration and ninety-
nine per cent perspiration."

But Edison was also a dreamer. From his earliest childhood he was fascinated by the secrets of nature. "Nature is full of mysteries," he often said. He brooded on these mysteries and tried to understand the secrets and figure out what he could do with them. He enjoyed thinking. "There are few things people won't do to avoid the labor of thinking," Edison said. "Unfortunately, thinking is the hardest work in the world for those who have not formed the habit. But thinking can give excitement and pleasure."

Edison could not imagine being bored. As he loved to think, he also loved to work. On his seventy-fifth birthday, he was asked what his philosophy of life was. "Work," he said, "bringing out the secrets of nature and applying them for the happiness of man." On that occasion he said that he had enough inventions in mind to keep him busy for another hundred years.

Edison suffered many privations in his early life and he knew disappointment and defeat, but he never thought of feeling sorry for himself. "You might as well look on the bright side," he said. He ascribed some of his remarkable power of concentration to his deafness. "Think of all the nonsense I haven't had to listen to by not being able to hear it," he said.

Thomas Alva Edison at eighty

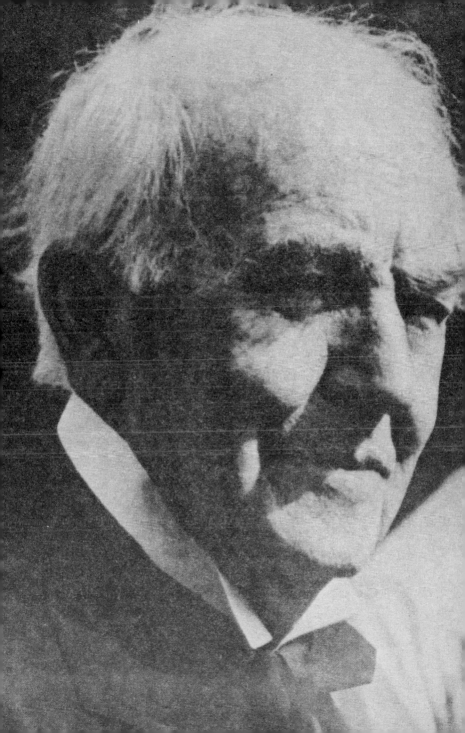

Edison took pride in his accomplishments when his inventions succeeded and benefited others. He understood the importance of publicity to bring his useful work to the attention of the public. But he was always modest. He appreciated the honors given him but would have worked on without them, or without recognition of any kind.

Few men who ever lived had more honors showered on them than Edison. In his library at Glenmont a large glass case was set up to hold his dozens of medals and decorations. Edison was once asked if he would put them on public display. "I have no objection," he said, "but I can't imagine who would be interested in looking at them." Then began a search for the key to the glass case. Edison couldn't remember where he had put it. It was never found and the case had to be broken open. Edison was then asked to identify the medals and say something about the occasions when they had been awarded. He couldn't remember what they were or how he had happened to be so honored or where or when.

Edison met and knew most of the great figures in the world during his lifetime, and dined with kings and princes. But he was never able to believe that there was anything special about himself. He was interested in people, not their titles. Even after he got to be an old man, he could not understand why anybody deferred to him. When the president of the Pennsylvania Railroad once insisted on carrying Edison's valise off the train, Edison was amazed. He couldn't understand why the man had done it.

He was humble about his work. "I have tried so many things I thought were true and found out that I was wrong that I have quit being too sure about anything," he said. "All I can do is to try everything to prove my idea is right and give it up only when I am sure it won't work."

While Edison was both modest and humble, he was not much influenced by the opinions of others. He was an original person who thought and acted as he felt he should. It was impossible for him to imitate or conform. He would not be bound by tradition or rules.

Edison had unusual ideas about eating. For such a big man he did not eat very much and he felt that most illness was due to overeating. He also felt that people should eat many different kinds of things. "I wish I never had to eat the same thing twice," Edison said. "The world is full of a variety of food and we ought to try all of it." Edison ate everything except squash. He once said that anything that went down as easily as squash couldn't do you any good!

After Edison became famous, he was honored at many luncheons and dinners and receptions. He often carried his own dinner to a banquet in a

171

tin box. While everybody else ate through six or eight rich courses, Edison would dine on sardines, spinach, tomatoes, crackers and a glass of milk.

Edison chewed tobacco and smoked a large number of cigars every day, but he had a horror of cigarettes. He was one of the first people to declare that cigarettes were dangerous.

Edison felt that people wasted too much precious time in sleeping. He could sleep anywhere, and often took catnaps in the middle of a conversation. "Loss of sleep never hurt anybody," he declared, and he told President Coolidge that he was sleeping too much. Edison's own sleep habits were curious. Sometimes he would sleep twenty-four hours without waking up. He thought nothing of throwing himself down on the damp ground or the soiled floor of the laboratory or curling up on a pile of sewer pipe to sleep. Although he worked much and slept little for sixty years of his life, he was rarely ill. He continued to look, act and be youthful. It never occurred to him to stop work or retire.

Edison did not believe in worry. He was too busy to worry about what might happen. He was more interested in *making* something happen. When things did not work out to suit him, he did not worry about what *had* happened. "I have no interest in spilt milk," he said.

As a leader, Edison inspired loyalty in the men

Edison as he appeared in 1888 after seventy-two sleepless hours of work on an improved phonograph

who worked for him. He asked more than they could give, and they all wanted to please him. He worked alongside them and had endless patience. But his disposition was changeable. He loved jokes. He whistled, sang and laughed at work. But he also had a quick temper. He could not forgive people who slighted their work or did not insist, as he did, on the highest quality of performance. When he became angry, he would pound the table and shout. Since he was deaf, the other person would have to shout back. On bad days there was a good deal of noise around the laboratories.

When Edison was in a bad temper, most people tried to stay out of his way. He would march through the factory firing people right and left for any reason or no reason. Fortunately, his trusted employees were usually able to hide, or Edison was so absent-minded, that before morning he would forget all about having fired them. Men who had been fired by "the boss" often returned to their machines the next day, and Edison never remembered anything about it.

Although Edison was so absent-minded that he forgot the time of day, the day of the week and even his own name, he never forgot a man's face. He could recognize the faces and call the names of men he had not seen for a quarter of a century.

Between 1869 and 1910, the inventor's years of greatest achievement, Edison applied for 1,328 separate and distinct patents. He made many inventions that he did not attempt to patent— inventions that he left unpatented and simply gave to the public. There was little in the world that did not interest him. He could carry on many different types of research at the same time. He could work on unimportant things with the same zest and enthusiasm he gave to important things. For several weeks at one time, he was interested in creating a doll that could talk. Edison spent considerable time playing with his phonographic dolls.

Edison was a man of ideas. But he did not believe that there was anything unusual about his ability to have ideas. He said that anybody could have ideas who was willing to observe, study and think. He believed that people should start as early as possible to look at the world and nature and to draw conclusions about what they saw. "Thinking is a habit," he said over and over. "If you do not learn to think when you are young, you may never learn." He never denied that he made guesses. Guesswork or hunches, proved by experiment, may become invention, he said.

"Imagination supplies the ideas," Edison said. "Technical knowledge carries them out." Unless ideas are carried out, they are useless.

"I always keep within a few feet of the earth's surface all the time," Edison said. "I never let my thoughts run up higher than the Himalayas!"

Edison believed in education. Self-educated, he knew the value of learning. "Education isn't play—and it can't be made to look like play," he said. "It is hard, hard work. But it can be made interesting work."

Edison believed in God. "I tell you that no person can be brought into close contact with the mysteries of nature or make a study of chemistry without being convinced that behind it all there is a supreme intelligence."

Edison believed in the future. "I think the world is on the eve of grand and immense discoveries before whose glory the record of the past will fade," he said. Of the future he also said: "We shall have no better conditions in the future if we are satisfied with all those we have at present. Restlessness is discontent and discontent is the first necessity of progress. Show me a thoroughly satisfied man—I will show you a failure." Edison had no patience with people who felt that the world had gone about as far as it could go. "There is far more opportunity than there is ability," he said.

Edison believed in America. When he was decorated by other governments, he always said that he felt the honor was not for him but for his country. When Mina Edison tried to persuade him to wear the Legion of Honor ribbon France had awarded him, he refused. He did not want to be different from his countrymen. "They might jolly me about it," he said. When Edison was awarded the Congressional Medal of Honor in 1928, he was called the most useful American citizen.

In June 1961 Thomas Edison took his place among the American immortals in the Hall of Fame at New York University. Perhaps no one has more truly deserved this honor. He typified the American ideal in his determination to harness the secrets of nature for the benefit of all people everywhere. He recognized that the measure of life is not what we get but what we give.

Wherever the tiniest filament of electric light glimmers in darkness, Thomas Alva Edison's work lives after him.

Author's Note

The more I learn about Edison, the more I admire him. He was a doer, and although he literally changed the world, he remained the same human being—modest, stubborn, excitable and always full of fun. We take many of Edison's legacies to us for granted, but few people have contributed more to the comfort, convenience and sheer entertainment in our lives.

Edison entered on his lifework when he was very young and his career covered a long span of years, so that he became a legend during his own lifetime. He had an outstanding personality and always attracted writers and journalists. Edison knew the value of public interest and confidence in his projects, and he was able to dramatize his experiments so that people could understand them. Unlike many scientists, he welcomed attention to his work and was available to the working press. A great quantity of material about his life and his inventions, much of it based on first-hand interviews and Edison's own notes, is now stored in libraries.

Edison was a colorful storyteller, and reports of his recollections of the same incident may differ from one source to another. Conversations in this book are either quoted directly from participants or reconstructed on the basis of long study of the inventor's character and nature and the perusal of numerous sources. I made a special effort to seek out books written for young readers during Edison's lifetime and published with his knowledge.

Finally I am grateful to Norman R. Speiden, supervisory museum curator of the Edison National Historic Site, West Orange, New Jersey, and to Marvin Geller, electrical engineer, for their detailed comments about the text.

Index

References to illustrations are in *italics.*

184

About the Author

Margaret Cousins was born in Munday, Texas, and grew up in Dallas. She was graduated from the University of Texas at Austin, which recently named her Distinguished Alumna, and was awarded the degree of Doctor of Literature by William Woods College of Fulton, Missouri, in 1980. For many years she pursued an editorial career in New York City, where she was managing editor of *Good Housekeeping* and *McCall's* magazines, and fiction editor of *Ladies' Home Journal*. At the same time she contributed short stories, essays, and poetry to other popular magazines. Among her other books for young readers are: *Ben Franklin of Old Philadelphia* and *Uncle Edgar and the Reluctant Saint*. She now lives in San Antonio, Texas.